Pass the 63

BY

Robert Walker

FIRST BOOKS

©2004 Robert Walker

Cover designed by Kenny Kaiser.
Interior designed by Masha Shubin.

NASSA Statements of Policy and Model Rules reprinted with permission.

ISBN 0-912301-55-4

Publisher: First Books

www.firstbooks.com

Printed in the United States of America

Table of Contents

PASS THE 63

INTRODUCTION

Congratulations!

Presumably, you have just passed the Series 6, 7, or 65 exam, all of which represent a major achievement on your part. At this point you have passed the "national" part of your securities licensing requirements.

But—guess what—you will also be working in particular states, and those states have licensing requirements, too. At this point your Series 6, 7, or 65 has basically been impounded by the securities Administrator of your state and will not be released for your professional use until you pass a rather difficult exam called the Series 63.

Why all the fuss?

Well, the states get real nervous whenever somebody tries to sell securities. It would be very easy for some fly-by-night operation to set up shop in a state, sell a bunch of worthless stock, then take the proceeds and run away, leaving investors holding the bag. States don't take kindly to that sort of thing. They're out to protect the average investor from fraud and unethical practices in the purchase and sale of securities.

So in the 1950's securities regulators from around the country passed the Uniform Securities Act. This model legislation serves as a template that the state regulators use to draft securities laws within their states, keeping all the laws fairly "uniform." Notice how we don't get real creative with the language here. If the act is designed to keep the <u>securities</u> laws of the states <u>uniform</u>, we simply name it the <u>Uniform</u> <u>Securities</u> Act. When somebody represents an investment adviser, we call that person an <u>investment adviser</u> *representative*. When somebody issues securities, guess what we call them?

An issuer.

We also use some words you might not be familiar with—like *contumacy, adjudication, enjoin,* and *non-exempt*—but we'll get to that later. For now, let's take a look at the story behind the Series 63 and the Uniform Securities Act.

The major concern of a state securities regulator is that some fly-by-night operation will try to set up shop just long enough to dump a bunch of worthless stock on the average investor, take the proceeds, and flee the state. So, whenever somebody even proposes to issue a security, the state defines that person as an "issuer." Now all the rules on "issuers" spelled out in the USA apply to this person. This person is going to have to register the securities before they can be sold in the state. Investors have to receive a disclosure document that doesn't just make big promises but also details the risks involved with purchasing this—or any—security. The state might even force these issuers to establish an escrow account whose proceeds will not be released by the state until the issuer has raised the amount they're attempting to raise. If the issuer is registering the stock at the federal (SEC) level, the state often wants to see the same stuff they're showing the SEC. If the company is in shaky condition, or if they're going to pay the underwriters way too much money, or if the whole thing just doesn't pass the smell test, the issuer might not even get to sell the stock in the state.

See, selling securities isn't a right. It's a privilege. If you want the privilege of using other people's money to finance your business, you have to earn that privilege. Which means you pay your fees and file all the paperwork required by the state. And—above all—you make sure that you do nothing unethical or fraudulent, unless you care to spend a few years in jail.

Remember, the criminal penalty for fraud at the state level can go up to a fine of $5,000, three years in jail, or both.

So, the states expect these issuers to be on their best behavior when they come into the state trying to raise money by selling stock.

In fact, the states expect <u>everybody</u> to be on his/her best behavior when issuing or selling this stock. The investment advisers, broker-dealers, and agents pushing this stock on residents of the state also need to be registered and also need to watch their P's and Q's. Unless, of course, they want to donate $5,000 to the state coffers and spend three years getting acquainted with a 285-pound, heavily tattooed cell mate serving time for assault with a deadly weapon.

No thanks, right?

So if your firm is an investment adviser or a broker-dealer doing business in that state, or if you're an individual representing those firms, you have to file paperwork, pay your fees, and be on your best behavior.

Again, selling securities and financial advice is a privilege, not a right, and it's a privilege that can be taken away by the Administrator any time it's in the public interest and provides protection to the average investor.

So, the state securities Administrator is first of all going to regulate all the firms and the representatives of the firms that have set up shop within the state. If I'm the Administrator for Illinois, I'm regulating the investment advisers and broker-dealers, as well as the representatives of those firms, doing business in Illinois. I don't give a rip about the firms doing business in Wisconsin, right? They don't even show up on my radar screen until they start selling securities/advice to folks in Illinois. If a firm doing business in Wisconsin wants to sell securities or advice to someone in Illinois, the key question I have is "To whom are they trying to sell?" If they just want to sell to professional or institutional investors (banks, insurance companies, mutual funds, and pension funds), then I won't even make them register as a broker-dealer or investment adviser in Illinois. If this Wisconsin firm pulls any funny stuff, I'll go after them with everything I've got, but I don't have to provide as much protection to the sophisticated, well-funded institutional investors in my state as I have to provide to the average investor. So, if the firm wants to sell to more than 5 "little guys" or non-institutional investors, then the Wisconsin firm WILL have to register as a broker-dealer or investment adviser in the state of Illinois, because I provide more protection to the little guy.

What's the big deal with being defined by and forced to register with the Administrator?

Well, look at your current situation. How has your life been impacted now that you have been defined as an "agent" of a licensed "broker-dealer" or "investment adviser"? Suddenly, there are fees to pay, paperwork to be filed, and several tough exams to be passed with no small effort on your part. Even after you get your license you'll be subject to more fees, paperwork, and continuing education requirements.

Wouldn't it be great if the state you operate in told you that you were excluded from the definition of "registered representative"? Then all this stuff would be somebody else's problem, not yours.

Nobody wants to be defined and regulated under the Uniform Securities Act. But if they haven't been granted an **exemption**/exclusion, then the USA does, in fact, apply to them, and they do, in fact, have to mind their P's and Q's.

So if the firm or the representative of the firm <u>does not</u> have an office in a particular state, they often do not have to register in that state. If they sell to institutions, they do not have to register in that state. But, if they sell to more than a few non-institutional investors, they will have to register in that state.

Fascinating stuff, isn't it?

Okay, so securities firms (broker-dealers, investment advisers) have to be properly registered or properly excused (exempted/excluded) from registration. The individuals working at such firms (agents, investment adviser representatives) have to be properly registered at the state level, or properly excused from registration. And, securities also have to be properly registered or properly excused from the arduous process of registration.

Some securities have to be registered. Some don't. Those that don't have to be registered have been granted exemptions from registration. Guess what we call them?

Exempt securities. Exempt means *excused.*

Now, see if you can guess what we call those securities that have to be registered because they DON'T have an exemption.

Non-exempt securities. Non-exempt means *not excused.*

The registration requirements apply to all securities, except to all the securities they don't apply to. If the requirements don't apply, that's an exempt security. If the requirements do apply, the security didn't qualify for an exemption and is, therefore, called a non-exempt security.

You're sure you want to get your license, right?

Just checking.

Anyway, lots of securities are exempt from registering with the SEC. Government bonds, municipal bonds, bank securities, small business investment company securities, non-profit securities, and securities that mature in 270 days or less—like commercial paper and bankers acceptances—are all exempt from registering under the Securities Act of 1933. So, if the security is exempt at the federal level, it is automatically exempt at the state level. The states can never have higher standards than the feds. NSMIA (National Securities Markets Improvement Act of 1996) made sure of that. The SEC (federal) recognizes a class of securities as *federal covered* because of NSMIA. These securities are either granted an exemption from federal registration or covered exclusively at the federal level. If the security is exempt at the federal level, it is automatically exempt at the state level. And other federal covered securities are covered only at the federal level. An example of the these would be IBM or GE. These corporations have to register their stock with the SEC, but they don't have to register with all the states because they are covered at the federal level only—federal covered. If the stock trades on a recognized exchange or is called a "NASDAQ" stock, then it is federal covered. Its registration is handled by the SEC (federal), which is actually plenty to deal with, as it turns out. Mutual funds/investment company securities are federal covered, as are shares of public utilities. So, if the security is exempt at the federal level, or covered exclusively at the federal level, it does not have to be registered at the state level because it is federal covered—covered by the federal organization known as the SEC.

Which means if the security is *not* federal covered, then it <u>does</u> have to be registered at the state level. Companies trading on the OTC Bulletin Board and the Pink Sheets have to register at the state level. There isn't as much information on these companies, so they'll have to register with the states by **coordination**, **filing**, or **qualification**, which will be discussed later.

The US Government is an exempt <u>*issuer*</u>. Commercial paper is an exempt <u>*security*</u>. That's why neither a T-bond nor a piece of GE commercial paper would have to be registered. So, if an agent sold either security and it turned out the security wasn't registered, that's okay.

In fact, that's how it's supposed to go down. Those securities are exempt from registration. If the agent is doing business in Florida, **she** needs to be registered in the state of Florida. **She** needs to be registered in every state in which **she** is doing business. But an Illinois revenue bond would not have to be registered in any state. Therefore, if she is properly registered as an agent in Florida and sells an unregistered IL Revenue Bond, good for her! She made a nice sale of an exempt security as a properly registered agent in Florida.

<u>She</u> has to be registered. The exempt security does not.

If she sells an unregistered non-exempt security, *that's* a problem. Non-exempt securities have to be registered. Why?

They have no excuse, no exemption.

If the agent accidentally sold a non-exempt security that turned out not to be registered in the state, she committed a prohibited act. If she knew the stock was unregistered and sold it anyway, she committed fraud.

Fraud is the willful attempt to deceive someone for financial gain.

Don't do it.

And if you do do it, please don't get caught.

We'll discuss all the stuff you can't do later, but for now just remember that fraud is willful deception. Prohibited acts are things you just don't want to do.

So, how much power does the state securities Administrator have, anyway?

A lot.

The Administrator can investigate both inside and outside the state. If you commit fraud in Fort Myers, Florida, the Administrator can chase you all the way to Walla Walla, Washington. And, if the official in Florida doesn't feel like flying, he/she can just send the subpoena to the Administrator in Washington, who will be happy to greet you at the local airport with the out-of-state subpoena for everybody's convenience. Just look for the guy in the dark suit holding up the big sign with the word "Busted!" across it in red ink. If you're formally found to have violated provisions of the USA, you can have your license **denied, suspended** or **revoked**, which is bad. And, the Administrator just loves to publish violations in newspapers, websites, or any other embarrassing, far-reaching forum he can think of.

Now that you've been in trouble with the folks in Florida, good luck trying to set up shop in other states. Remember, your license can be **denied**, **suspended** or **revoked** in a state based on the trouble you got into in any other state. In fact, if you were busted by a foreign banking authority or were convicted of any securities-related misdemeanor or any felony, your license can be denied, suspended, and revoked in any other state.

So, let's talk about what the Administrator can NOT do.

The Administrator can not issue an injunction. Only a court can do that. And, the Administrator can not sentence a person to jail—again, only a court can do that. The Administrator can take you to court—but they have to go to the trouble of proving you guilty before a judge first.

Basically, don't mess with the Administrator, and the Administrator won't mess with you.

So, there IS a story behind all this stuff—it's not just a bunch of details out to make your life miserable. The state securities Administrators are trying to protect the average investor from fraud. They regulate everybody they need to regulate, and before they can do that they have to carefully define who does and does not fall under the various definitions spelled out in the Uniform Securities Act. You and your firm, obviously, both fall under some of the definitions of the Act, which is why you have to pass your state-level exam before you can use your license.

So, let's get down to details now and define the players as well as what they can and can't do. Ready?

Let's do it, anyway.

Agents Defined

Imagine trying to explain the game of baseball to someone who has absolutely no knowledge of the game. Terms that you have taken for granted since childhood would suddenly involve lots of tedious, complicated explanations. You would have to define the "pitcher" and the "catcher" so that the person unfamiliar with baseball would soon understand that the pitcher is not the catcher, and the catcher is not the pitcher. Neither one would be the first baseman, nor the shortstop, nor the left fielder, right? When the *batter* steps up to the *plate*, he gets four *balls* and three *strikes*.

What's a strike?

That's when he swings the *bat* and misses, or when he should have swung the bat and didn't.

Who decides when he should swing the bat?

An official called the *umpire*—we'll get to him later.

Are those the only two ways to get a strike?

Well, no, he could also swing the bat and hit the ball, but send the ball either behind him or too far to the left or right, which is a *foul ball*, also recorded as a strike.

So, he could strike out with foul balls?

No, the third strike triggering the official "strike out" could never be effected via a foul ball, unless the batter tried to bunt or somebody on the other team *catches* the foul ball—then he's *out*.

A strike out?

No, that's a *foul out*.

So, after the third strike—unless it's a foul ball—the batter is out?

Yes, except when the catcher drops the ball on the third strike. Then, the batter gets to run toward first base where he might—or might not—make it safely.

Why?

Cause that's a "dropped third strike."

And you thought baseball was simple!

Pretty simple to step on the field and start playing, but not so simple when you step off the field and try to define all the terminology and complex structure of rules. Well, the securities industry is even more complicated than the game of baseball, and before we can even begin to lay down all the complex rules and exemptions to the rules, we first have to define all the players and terminology. Only after clearly defining who is and isn't a *broker-dealer, agent,* or *investment adviser,* and what we mean by seemingly simple terms like "person" or "security" can we tell these broker-dealers, agents, advisers and other "persons" what they can and can't do when they're dealing with "securities."

Defining the players and basic terminology of the securities industry is a major focus of the Series 63 exam and one of the trickier aspects. So let's get started.

Agent

An agent is always an individual and always represents someone else. An agent can either represent a firm defined as a *broker-dealer,* or the agent can represent an entity known as an *issuer* of securities. That means that an agent is NOT a broker-dealer, and is NOT an issuer. Just like the pitcher is NOT the catcher, the shortstop, or the right fielder. So, if you get a test question asking, "Which of the following are agents?" you can eliminate any choice that starts off like this:

- a broker-dealer who . . .
- an issuer who . . .

Broker-dealers and issuers are NOT agents. The agent represents one of those two entities, but the agent is not one of those entities him or herself. Sort of like saying that Sammy Sosa plays for the Chicago Cubs. Sammy Sosa, however, is NOT the Chicago Cubs, even if he has been known to carry the team from time to time.

Sounds goofy, but if we don't establish who is and isn't an agent, how are we going to tell these agents what they can and can't do? In baseball you wouldn't be able to tell the shortstop to stay off the pitcher's mound until you first clarify that the shortstop is NOT the pitcher, and the pitcher sure isn't the shortstop.

Anyway, if the individual selling securities represents a broker-dealer, that individual is defined as an agent, end of story. However, an individual can also represent an issuer, and this is where it gets tricky. First of all, an issuer is anyone who actually issues or proposes to issue securities. In other words, as soon as you file paperwork announcing your intention to raise money by selling securities to investors, you're an "issuer" as defined by the Uniform Securities Act. Chances are, you hire a few individuals to help sell your securities. Sometimes these folks have to register as agents; sometimes, they do not have to register as agents.

As you probably recall from the Series 6, 7, or 65, many issuers are exempt from the Securities Act of 1933. If they're exempt, that means the filing requirements of that act simply do not apply to them. Well, the federal government came up with the Securities Act of 1933, so guess who got the first exemption?

That's right, the federal government. If it's a security issued by the U.S. Government, it's exempt from the Act of 1933's registration requirements. T-bills, T-notes, T-bonds, STRIPS, savings bonds, Ginnie Mae's . . . all exempt from the Act. So, if the individual represents the U.S. Government in selling their securities, that individual is NOT defined as an agent. If the individual represents the issuer of any of the following exempt securities, he/she is also excluded from the definition of "agent":

- municipal securities
- non-profits, i.e. church bonds
- state bank or savings and loan securities
- small business investment company securities
- banker's acceptances, commercial paper, promissory notes maturing 270 days or less
- foreign government securities (at national/federal level only)

So, if the individual represents the issuers of any of those exempt securities, the individual is NOT defined as an agent. The foreign government issuer requires some explanation, though. First of all, if the U.S. has diplomatic relations with the foreign government, any security issued by that foreign government is exempt. But we're talking about <u>national</u> governments only. The government of France is an exempt issuer; the government of Paris is *not* exempt or "non-exempt." Bonds issued by the federal/national government of Mexico are exempt; bonds issued by Mexico *City* are not.

See the pattern?

Good—now let's throw it out the window for our neighbors to the north, Canada. We're so close to our Canadian counterparts, that any <u>government</u> security issued way up north there is exempt. National, provincial (state), or local—all exempt. So the bonds issued by the city of Montreal are just as exempt as the bonds issued by the province/state of Quebec or the national government of Canada.

But for all the *other* countries, only the securities issued at the national/country-wide level are exempt.

Don't take it too far, though. There is no exemption for Canadian *corporations*. Only governments.

There are exempt <u>issuers</u>, and there are exempt <u>securities</u>. An exempt issuer would be the U.S. Government. An example of an exempt security would be a promissory note that matures in 270 days or less (banker's acceptance, commercial paper) as long as it's at least $50,000 in denomination and in the top three tiers of credit ratings. So, if the individual represents an issuer in a sale of exempt securities, that person is NOT an agent. You sell T-bonds for the US Government? Not an agent. But, if you sell T-bonds for a broker-dealer, you ARE an agent. You sell commercial paper for the issuer of the commercial paper? Not an agent. You sell commercial paper for a broker-dealer? You ARE an agent.

Remember, if the individual represents the broker-dealer, that individual is always an agent. If the individual represents an exempt issuer, or if he/she represents an issuer in selling an exempt security, he/she is not an agent.

So, there are exempt <u>issuers</u>, and there are exempt <u>securities</u>. General Electric, for example, is not an exempt issuer—they do, after all, have to register their stock with the SEC. But GE also sells some securities exempt from registration, like commercial paper. So, GE is a non-exempt issuer. Their common stock is non-exempt, meaning it has to be registered. But, their commercial paper does NOT have to be registered because it is an exempt security.

So, there are exempt issuers and there are exempt securities.

Then, you got your exempt *transactions*. If the transaction qualifies for one of many exemptions, then the individual representing the issuer will NOT be defined as an agent.

Let's start with unsolicited orders. If a customer decides to call up an individual and request the opportunity to purchase securities, then the sales person really didn't prompt the customer to do anything, did he? That makes a huge difference to the state securities Administrator. See, the Administrator is out to protect the average investor from being *sold*. Individuals have the right to *buy* securities with their own free will—it's only when sales people start pushing securities on the public that the Administrator sits up and takes notice. So if it's an *unsolicited order* and the individual represents an <u>issuer</u>, that individual is NOT defined as an agent.

If the individual is representing an <u>issuer</u> when selling to a financial institution, that's also an exempt transaction, so the individual would NOT be defined as an agent under the Uniform Securities Act when representing an <u>issuer</u> and selling to banks, savings & loans, thrifts, or credit unions.

Let's say you work for Coca-Cola® selling Coca-Cola® stock to Coca-Cola® employees and you don't charge commissions. If so, you would not be defined as an agent. If you got commissions, you would be, but since you don't get commissions, you're not defined as an agent, just an employee of Coca-Cola® doing his or her job.

There are also individuals working for broker-dealers who are either not defined as agents at all or not required to register as agents. Technically, someone who is not defined as an agent has been granted an **exclusion**, whereas someone who simply doesn't have to register has been granted an **exemption**. But, the test will almost certainly not split hairs with you on that point. Whether the individual does not register due to an exclusion or due to an exemption is not really what the exam is after—the exam just wants you to know who does and doesn't have to register.

Partners and officers of the broker-dealer are not agents, unless they start selling securities. That's one of the few rules that actually make perfect sense, so let's enjoy it while we can. If they aren't selling, they aren't agents.

The Administrator in Illinois will let an agent registered in Wisconsin do business with an existing client just visiting the state

These folks are AGENTS:

- Any individual who represents a broker-dealer (doesn't matter what they sell) with an office in the state
- Any individual who represents an issuer if the issuer is <u>non</u>-exempt, if the security is <u>non</u>-exempt, or if the transaction is <u>non</u>-exempt. (if the issuer, security, or transaction doesn't qualify for an exclusion/excuse/exemption, then the individual IS defined as an agent)

These folks are NOT AGENTS:

- Broker-dealers
- Issuers
- Officers and directors of B/D's who do NOT sell
- Individual <u>with NO office in the state</u> selling to an existing customer who is <u>NOT a resident</u> of the state
- Individuals who represent exempt <u>issuers</u> like:
- U.S. Government
- Municipalities
- Banks
- Foreign governments at the national/federal level
- Individuals who represent issuers selling exempt <u>securities</u>:
- Commercial paper
- Banker's acceptances
- Individuals who represent issuers in exempt <u>transactions</u>:
- Unsolicited orders
- Sales to employees of company with no commission charged
- Transactions with institutional investors
- Transactions with financial institutions
- Transactions with underwriters

NOTE: So, the agent is ALWAYS an individual and is NEVER a broker-dealer or an issuer. If the agent represents a broker-dealer that person is ALWAYS an agent. But, if the individual represents an issuer, you have to see if they qualify for an exemption/exclusion based on the issuer, security, or transaction of Illinois without defining that individual as an agent in Illinois. That customer is not a resident of Illinois since he or she is only here temporarily (30 days or less), so the sales rep is NOT an agent in Illinois. If that customer hangs around too long, we've got a different story, but if he/she is here temporarily (not a resident of the state) the sales rep is not considered an agent in Illinois.

What's the big deal with being defined as an agent? Well, once the Administrator has defined you as an agent in the state, now you have to register in the state. And registration costs time and money, which is why so many people kicked and screamed to get an exemption from this inconvenience. Wouldn't you like an exemption from filling out paperwork, paying fees, and passing some test called the Series 63?

But, if you don't have some kind of exemption, you'll have to register as an agent. Someone without an exemption is called "non-exempt" in the language of the Uniform Securities Act. So if you see the word "non-exempt," remember that that person or that security has <u>no excuse</u> or exemption to hide behind. The rules apply to non-exempt people and securities; they don't apply to exempt people and securities.

Are we having fun yet?

Super.

You'll need to do lots of practice questions before your exam, so let's do some practice questions right now on who IS and is NOT an agent.

Ready?

Let's do 'em anyway.

1. **Which of the following is defined as an agent?**
    A. a broker-dealer with an office in the state who sells exempt securities
    B. a broker-dealer with no office in the state who sells non-exempt securities
    C. an individual who represents the US Government in selling T-bonds to wealthy investors
    D. an individual who represents a broker-dealer selling exempt securities

2. **Which of the following are not agents?**
    A. broker-dealer who sells exempt securities
    B. broker-dealer who sells nonexempt securities
    C. individual with no office in the state who sells to a customer staying 25 days in the state
    D. all of the above

3. **None of the following is an agent except**
    A. individual who sells Montreal revenue bonds on behalf of the issuer
    B. individual who represents XXY Corporation in selling XXY stock to XXY employees and charges no commissions
    C. individual who sells Mexico City revenue bonds on behalf of the issuer
    D. none of the above is an agent

Agents—Fraud and Other Prohibited Activities

Okay, now that we've defined what an agent is—and is not—let's talk about what these agents can and can not do. Something you aren't supposed to do is called a **prohibited practice**, whether you meant to do it or not. Prohibited practices can get your license **denied, suspended,** or **revoked**, which is bad. And, if you knew something was prohibited and did it anyway, it's not just prohibited, it could be considered **fraud**. People get fined and thrown in jail for committing fraud, which is also bad.

Fraud

Here is the legalistic version, pulled right from the USA itself:

Section 101. [Sales and Purchases.] It is unlawful for any person, in connection with the offer, sale, or purchase of any security, directly or indirectly
   (1)   to employ any device, scheme, or artifice to defraud,
   (2)   to make any untrue statement of a material fact or to omit to state a material fact necessary in order to make the statements made, in the light of the circumstances under which they are made, not misleading, or
   (3)   to engage in any act, practice, or course of business which operates or would operate as a fraud or deceit upon any person

Now, let's translate the above back into a language you are probably more familiar with—*English*.

What that legalese is saying is, "Don't lie, cheat, or steal from your customers when offering/selling securities to them." Material facts are the key—if the facts are material/important/relevant to the customer's decision, you can't misrepresent those facts or fail to provide them. If you do, you have probably committed fraud. Let's say you're trying to sell a brand new share of stock to a skeptical customer. You know this customer will hang up on you if you inform her that the company hasn't made a profit in any of the past three years, so you conveniently omit that material fact from your presentation.

Oops! Any time you *omit material information*, you have probably committed fraud, which is bad. If you omit material information or lie about material information, you're going to have the opportunity to donate $5,000 to the state and spend three years explaining your crime to a large cell mate serving 15 years for assault with a deadly weapon. Three years, five grand. Remember that.

What if the information is IM-material?

Then you should definitely omit it from your presentation to the customer. An IM-material fact would be the average height of GE's vice-presidents or the particular model of water cooler selected for the break room. If you omit that kind of irrelevant information, good for you—it should be omitted. And if you told the customer the company was painting their visitor lobby red, when, in fact, the color was mauve, so what? The customer can't come after you for that—it wasn't material information.

So fraud is basically the intentional/willful attempt to deceive someone for financial gain. If you lie about material facts or conceal them from customers, you have probably committed fraud, which is bad.

The law also says that fraud is not limited to judicial or case-law definitions —it can be established by statute, meaning if the governor and/or legislature defines something as fraud, guess what?

It's fraud.

Also remember that the penalties and sanctions for fraud include:

- administrative proceedings
- judicial injunctions
- criminal or civil prosecutions

So, fraud is bad. Really bad. If you deceive someone when selling securities, you could go to jail for **three years** and pay a fine up to **$5,000**, which is bad.

The rest of this stuff is all prohibited. That means, DON'T DO IT.

If you commit prohibited acts, you probably won't end up in jail, but you could easily end up having your license denied, suspended, or revoked.

Which is bad.

So these are most of the things to do and not do once you start work as an agent.

UNSUITABLE RECOMMENDATIONS

Investors trust agents to make suitable recommendations. High-rollers can afford to buy junk bonds and penny stocks, so if your customer is a high roller, go ahead and recommend risky investments. Look out, though, if you start recommending high-risk investments to senior citizens living on modest fixed incomes. A senior citizen living on a modest fixed income would probably put some money in a money market account, a high-grade corporate or government bond fund, or maybe a few select blue chip stocks, right? So, recommend what's appropriate to each individual customer; otherwise, you can get in trouble for making *unsuitable recommendations*. They don't all have to be profitable, but all your recommendations to clients must be suitable.

CHURNING

Of course, if you're an agent, all your customer's transactions generate a commission for you. That's right, whether your customer makes money or loses money, you get a commission when they buy and a commission when they sell.

Sounds like a pretty good deal, huh? So, the best way for you to make money is to get your customers buying and selling all day every day, right?

Yep, except that's a major no-no called *churning*. If you're pressuring customers to trade frequently just so you can pocket commissions, you can get busted for churning, which is bad.

THE DREADED A-WORD

To impress this skeptical customer, you tell her the security has been approved for sale, either by the SEC or the state securities Administrator.

Not! Securities are never "approved." Regulators <u>allow</u>, they don't *approve*.

ACCEPTING ORDERS ON BEHALF OF CUSTOMERS FROM A THIRD PARTY WITHOUT TRADING AUTHORIZATION

One of your best customers is too busy to call you, so he has his wife give you a ring. Buy 10,000 shares of ORCL at $15.75, fill or kill, she says.

What do you do?

Not a darned thing. Not until you've talked to your client. If the couple had a joint account with you, that would be different, but if it's an individual account, you can only accept orders from that individual. If that individual gives trading authorization to another individual—i.e., his wife—and you have that on paper, then it's okay. But a third party without authorization can't tell you what to do for your client's account.

UNAUTHORIZED BORROWING OF MONEY OR SECURITIES FROM A CUSTOMER.

> Hi, Mrs. Wilson. This is Ryan Reynolds, your smiling and dialing registered representative. Look, it's been a tough quarter for me, Ma'am, now that everybody's too chicken to buy stocks and all, and I was wondering if you could, like, spot me a few hundred bucks until payday?

Well, that conversation isn't going to happen, right?

An agent can not borrow money from a client, nor would he/she want to try. The only customer that an agent can borrow money from is a bank, since banks are in the business of loaning people money, as long as they can prove on paper they don't actually need it.

Commingling

Wouldn't it be fun to control one big account with millions of dollars of assets all mixed in together between you and your millionaire customers? Might be fun, but it's actually a big no-no called *commingling*. Assets have to be separate. You can put customer assets in a common trust, just make sure you don't put customer assets in with your own or your firm's assets. Keep it all nice and separated—customer stuff here, agent stuff here—and everybody's happy.

Deliberately failing to follow a customer's instructions

Here's another conversation that isn't going to happen:

> Hi, Mrs. Wilson, this is Ryan again. Remember when you told me to sell E-toys when it hit three bucks a share? Well, it hit three bucks a share, only guess what? I didn't sell it. Where's it trading at? Let me see . . . uh, looks like it's about to find support at twelve. No, *cents*. Hello? Mrs. Wilson?

Failure to follow your customers' instructions can get you in all kinds of trouble and is a prohibited practice. So, never would you want to not follow your customers' explicit instructions.

Failure to bring to the attention of agent's employing broker-dealer a customer's written complaints

If your customer gives you a written complaint should you A, take it to your supervisor or B, take it to the shredder? Always take written complaints to your supervisor, who can always take it to the shredder himself and probably needs the exercise. If it's in writing, you have to take it to your supervisor, who isn't going to be real happy to see it. But if you think he's mad now, see how he reacts when the firm gets fined and/or sanctioned because you "forgot" to tell him that Mrs. Wilson had written a dozen letters to express her displeasure with the firm.

Ouch.

Guaranteeing Customers a Profit; Guaranteeing Against a Loss

Oracle is such a great buy at fifteen, Mrs. Wilson, I tell you what I'm gonna do. If you end up losing anything on the deal, I'll personally refund your money. That's right, I guarantee you'll make money on this investment, Ma'am. No, you can't possibly lose. I guarantee it.

Not.

The word *guarantee* can be used in a very limited sense. The US Government guarantees payment on their T-bonds, which are issued by the folks at the Treasury Department with their fingers conveniently on the printing press. Insurance companies guarantee payment on fixed annuities, but you and your broker-dealer guarantee nothing.

Sharing Profits or Losses with Customers

Let's say your customer is hesitant about buying a stock you're sure is set to rally. To ease her mind you offer to go halvsies on the deal. You know, if the stock goes up, we split the gain, and if the stock goes down, we split the loss.

Not.

Only way an agent can *share* with a client is to have an approved joint account with that client, and only share in proportion to what the agent has invested. On the exam, make sure the agent has the customer's written authorization and that of the firm.

Misrepresenting Status of Customer Accounts

You finally talked Mrs. Wilson into buying 1,000 shares of XYZ at $15. Luckily, Mrs. Wilson is in the state of Washington visiting her sister Wilma when XYZ gets walloped the next day. Next day Mrs. Wilson gives you a call, with XYZ currently trading at $3 a share.

How's that stock you sold me doing there, young fella?

Just fine, Mrs. Wilson. Right about where we bought it.

That's a lie. The law would never call it a "lie," but the law would tell you not to misrepresent the status of a customer's account, no matter how tempting.

Mutual Fund Projections

Mrs. Wilson, this mutual fund has returned an average of 22% the past five years. Based on that performance, I expect it to do at least that well next year, probably better.

Oh no. No mutual fund projections, ever. Past performance does not guarantee future results, end of story.

MAKING RECOMMENDATIONS ON THE BASIS OF MATERIAL INSIDE INFORMATION

What if your sister, the CFO of a large public company, tells you that her firm is about to be purchased by an even larger public company? That should boost her company's stock price, so you call all your clients and tell them to hurry up and buy the stock.

Well, that's called *acting on material inside information* and you can get yourself into all kinds of trouble making recommendations based on such information. Wait until the information has become public unless you want to explain your actions to a roomful of ticked off regulators.

PROMISING TO PERFORM SERVICES WITHOUT INTENT OR ABILITY TO PERFORM THEM

You also shouldn't go around promising to perform services that you aren't likely or even able to perform. For example, if you're trying to land new customers, don't do so by promising to wash their car every Saturday for the next five years or balance their checkbook for them. That isn't your job, and you aren't likely to follow through, anyway.

SOLICITING ORDERS FOR UNREGISTERED, NON-EXEMPT SECURITIES

Break down those words. The security is "non-exempt," which means it has *no excuse* from registration. It must be registered, so if you're soliciting orders for securities that should be registered but are NOT registered, you're going to get yourself into all kinds of trouble. In fact, making sure that securities offered on the primary market are properly registered is one of the main goals of all this regulation. The states just don't like it when fly-by-night companies try to set up shop in some vacant strip mall just long enough to dump unregistered, bogus securities on the public, take the proceeds, and flee the state.

So, if the security has no exemption/excuse from registration (non-exempt), and you solicit orders for it—watch out! If you knew what you were doing and did it anyway, that could be considered fraud. And even if it was an "honest mistake," it's definitely a prohibited activity that can get your license denied, suspended, or revoked.

Which is bad.

All right. Let's look at a few practice questions on what you can and can't do as an agent.

4. **All of the following are prohibited practices except**
    A. depositing client funds into the agent's bank account
    B. recommending municipal bonds to a low-income investor with growth as an objective
    C. recommending municipal securities to a high-tax bracket investor within a retirement account
    D. not ignoring a customer's explicit instructions to not sell a security

5. **Minnie Mizerton is a risk-averse investor. Knowing Minnie's aversion to risk, an agent recommends that Minnie purchase T-bonds because they are riskless securities. What is true of this recommendation?**
    A. unsuitable, due to the high beta of treasury securities
    B. unsuitable and unlawful
    C. suitable and lawful
    D. suitable but unlawful due to interest rate risk retained by the investor

6. **Which of the following is an example of fraud?**
    A. an agent deliberately omits an immaterial fact when selling a security in order to avoid distracting the customer
    B. a customer claims that an agent sold an unsuitable security
    C. an agent deliberately omits a material fact when selling a security
    D. all of the above

7. **All of the following are prohibited acts except**
    A. an agent informs clients that she has been approved by the Administrator to recommend securities
    B. an agent shares commissions with other agents at the firm
    C. an agent deliberately fails to follow a customer's explicit instructions
    D. an agent promises to clean a client's bathroom every Saturday for the next 11 years if the client will purchase 1,000 shares of XYZ

8. **All of the following activities are prohibited except**
    A. an agent solicits orders for unregistered, non-exempt securities
    B. an agent solicits orders for unregistered, exempt securities
    C. an agent places a client's funds and securities into the agent's account with no intention of replacing them
    D. an agent places a client's funds and securities into the agent's account with every intention of replacing them at his earliest convenience

9. **All of the following are either fraudulent or prohibited except**
    A. telling a client that a security will be exchange-listed when the agent has no knowledge of that fact
    B. marking up a security by $1.00 and telling the client the markup is 25 cents
    C. failing to state all facts about an issuer when selling unregistered exempt securities
    D. offering to give a client her money back if a recommended security does not appreciate in value over the next 90 days

10. **Which of the following activities is fraudulent?**
    A. unwittingly accepting an order for an unregistered, nonexempt security
    B. marking up a security by $1.00 and telling the client the markup is 25 cents
    C. failing to state all facts about an issuer when selling unregistered, exempt securities
    D. all of the above

11. Which of the following activities is/are considered unethical?
   A. charging commissions that exceed industry standards with client's written consent
   B. charging markups that are higher than usual with the client's written consent
   C. indicating to clients that the agent has earned an MBA from the University of Chicago, when, in fact, the agent has only completed a BA
   D. all of the above

12. Which of the following are considered dishonest or unethical practices?
   A. an agent discloses the current yield of a mutual fund without clearly explaining the difference between current yield and total return
   B. an agent states that an investment company's performance is similar to that of a savings account, CD, or other bank deposit account without disclosing that the shares of the investment company are not guaranteed or insured by the FDIC or any other governmental agency
   C. an agent states that a government bond mutual fund portfolio holds securities guaranteed against default by the U.S. Government without also disclosing other risks such as interest rate risk
   D. all of the following

13. Which of the following are true concerning criminal penalties?
   A. there is no statute of limitations for securities fraud
   B. the statute of limitations for securities fraud is 2 years from discovery or 3 years from the alleged event, whichever comes first
   C. ignorance of the law/rule has no bearing in criminal proceedings
   D. the maximum penalty is 3 years in jail, $5,000 fine or both

Broker-Dealers Defined

Always remember—and please never forget:

AN AGENT IS NEVER A BROKER-DEALER, AND A BROKER-DEALER IS NEVER AN AGENT.

Not that you woke up this morning thinking otherwise; it's just that the Series 63 is somewhat obsessive when it comes to making sure you know that, so once again:

AN AGENT IS NEVER A BROKER-DEALER, AND A BROKER-DEALER IS NEVER AN AGENT.

An agent is always an individual. You are about to become an agent, right? You're not about to become a firm. A broker-dealer is a firm. You might be called a "broker" at the firm, but that's just shorthand for "stock broker," a term not used by the exam. The exam talks about agents, or investment representatives, because the exam is all about stodgy, legalistic language nobody ever actually uses.

A broker-dealer is a firm. The registered representatives smiling and dialing for the firm are agents. The exam might refer to the sales reps as *registered representatives*, *investment representatives*, or *agents*. In any case, the exam is talking about an individual. A broker-dealer is an entity, a business.

So, if the question asks something like, "Which of the following are agents?" you can eliminate any choice that starts out, "A broker-dealer who . . ."

Eliminate it.

The unskilled test taker will read the rest of the sentence, which might be something as annoying as:

. . . a broker-dealer properly registered in a neighboring state as well as the state in which the offer either originated or was accepted in the transference of non-exempt, properly registered securities for value.

You don't have time to read all that nonsense. Remember, as soon as you read, "A broker-dealer who . . ." you can stop right there. Agents are never broker-dealers, and broker-dealers are never agents.

Just like the right fielder isn't the shortstop, and the shortstop isn't the right fielder.

Okay, so what the heck IS a broker-dealer, then?

A broker-dealer is a firm *in the business of effecting transactions for others or for its own account*. See, it's an either-or situation, which is why the term **broker-dealer** is hyphenated. On a particular transaction, the firm could act as a broker and charge a commission, or act as a dealer and make a markup/markdown. In the business of effecting transactions for others (broker) or for its own account (dealer).

Agents only effect transactions for others. They are not broker-*dealers*. They don't have the authority or capacity to deal securities. They help people buy and sell them, that's all.

Would you like to deal securities? Would you like to buy 100,000 shares of some stock and then see how much buyers would be willing to pay for them later on?

You'd probably rather just pick up the phone and see if you can help your firm sell some of those nice securities to their nice clients at no risk to yourself, right?

That's why you're going to be an **agent**. You'll be working for a **broker-dealer**.

Okay, now that we've belabored that point, let's look at all the folks who look like broker-dealers on the surface, but actually turn out to be excluded from the definition upon closer examination.

THE FOLLOWING PLAYERS ARE NOT BROKER-DEALERS, EVER!

- agents
- issuers
- banks/trust companies

So, if the test question asks, "Which of the following are broker-dealers?" you can eliminate any choices that start out, "An agent who . . ." or, "An issuer who . . ." Agents, issuers, banks, trusts, S&L's . . . those folks are NOT broker-dealers. If they were broker-dealers, guess what we'd call them?

Broker-dealers.

So those folks aren't broker-dealers by definition. You have to look a little closer to find the others, who sure look like broker-dealers but end up escaping the definition.

Let's say the firm is properly registered as a broker-dealer in the state of Wisconsin. They have no office in Illinois, so at this point, what does the state securities Administrator for Illinois care about this broker-dealer in Wisconsin?

Not a rip, right?

So, this Wisconsin firm then wants to do business with some folks in Illinois.

Okay, now the IL securities Administrator looks up from his desk and asks an assistant exactly whom this Wisconsin firm wants to sell to in Illinois. Turns out the only folks the Wisconsin firm wants to deal with are banks, S&L's, trust companies, insurance companies, investment companies, and pension plans in Illinois.

Hmm, those folks usually have millions of dollars to invest and hire professional investors to manage their risk. Pretty sophisticated and able to smell fraud a mile away, right? Do I, as the securities Administrator for the state of Illinois, really have to spend my time protecting sophisticated institutional investors like that?

No.

If I find out somebody's been defrauding these institutional investors, I'll get involved in a heartbeat. But, if this firm properly registered in Wisconsin only wants to deal with these big multimillion-dollar institutional clients, I don't see any need to make them register in my state. So, they're exempt from registration, which means they don't have to register and are very happy about that.

The Administrator licenses people so he can monitor them in order to protect the average investor from fraud. The big guys don't need the same level of protection. Doesn't mean that folks can sell fraudulently to institutionals; just means that the institutionals don't have to be protected quite as much. No different from how closely a parent would watch a 2-year-old child as opposed to a 13-year-old child. Bottom line is that nobody messes with your children, but you have to watch out for the 2-year-old at all times, whereas, the 13-year-old can watch out for himself to a certain extent.

The Administrator will let an out-of-state firm do no more than 15 transactions with no more than 5 non-institutional/non-professional clients in order to qualify for a "de minimus exemption." *De minimus* is Latin for "so small it don't matter." So, the out-of-state firm can deal with as many pension funds or insurance companies as they want, but they can only make 15 offerings or perform 15 transactions per year with the little guys . . . unless they want to be defined as a broker-dealer in the other state. Which they don't. Be flexible on the test here. If the question is talking about "no more than 5 non-institutional clients" rather than focusing on the "15 transactions," I would go with it.

Just like with agents, if a broker-dealer is properly registered in Wisconsin and wants to sell to an existing customer just visiting in Illinois, the Illinois securities

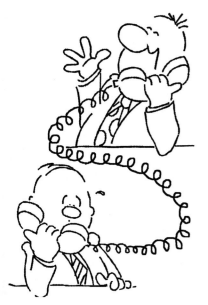

Administrator isn't going to define the firm as a broker-dealer in Illinois and therefore undergo the painful and expensive process of registration. Those existing customers are only in the other state for 30 days maximum, remember. More than 30 days, and now we've got a different situation entirely.

So if you're an issuer, right there you are NOT a broker-dealer by definition, because broker-dealers aren't issuers, and issuers aren't broker-dealers. Agents aren't broker-dealers, **ever**, as we've pointed out a couple of times. And, if you're a bank you are, therefore, NOT defined as a broker-dealer.

So banks and issuers are not broker-dealers by definition. Pension funds, investment companies, and insurance companies are also not defined as broker-dealers but are defined rather as *pension funds*, *investment companies*, and *insurance companies*, respectively.

Are we having fun yet?

Good!

14. **Which of the following are broker-dealers?**
    A.   an issuer of non-exempt, unregistered securities maturing in 270 days or less
    B.   a bank that invests more than 20% of total assets in securities
    C.   a firm that trades securities for its own account or the accounts of its customers
    D.   an agent who represents a broker-dealer in a non-exempt transaction

15. **Which of the following broker-dealers must register in the state of Kentucky?**
    A.   a broker-dealer properly registered in Ohio who sells securities to 17 pension plans located in Kentucky with more than $5,000,000 in assets
    B.   a broker-dealer registered in New Mexico who sells securities to 100 banks, trust companies, and S&L's in Kentucky.
    C.   a broker dealer with an office in Kentucky effects transactions only with banks and insurance companies located in Kentucky
    D.   a broker dealer with no office in the state of Kentucky sells to an existing customer not a resident of the state

16. **Which of the following persons would be defined as broker-dealers in the state?**
    A.   an agent selling promissory notes maturing in more than 12 months
    B.   a bank selling products insured by the FDIC
    C.   a firm with no office in the state that effects transactions with 7 pension funds in the state
    D.   a firm with no office in the state that effects transactions with 7 non-accredited investors who are residents of the state

THIS IS A BROKER-DEALER

- a firm—not an agent—in the business of effecting transactions in securities for accounts of others or its own account

THESE PERSONS ARE NOT BROKER-DEALERS

- agents*
- issuers*
- banks, trust companies*
- persons with NO OFFICE IN THE STATE who effect transactions exclusively with or through**:
- insurance companies
- investment companies
- banks
- savings institutions
- trust companies
- financial institutions or institutional buyers
- pension or profit-sharing trusts
- existing customers not residents of the state

* excluded from the definition of a broker-dealer, no matter where they operate

** these firms are probably broker-dealers in the state where they are located, but not required to register in the states where the "big guys" are located.

INVESTMENT ADVISERS AND IA REPRESENTATIVES DEFINED

For whatever reason, I'm really good at picking stocks. I've been known to make 50, 60, even 70% returns in a year. Pretty soon everybody's asking me my advice all the time. It gets to where I can't eat lunch in peace without somebody wanting to know my latest stock tips.

So, finally, I decide if I'm going to be bombarded with requests for my expert opinion, I might as well get paid for it. I print up business cards, and I start making investment recommendations to people, charging them a fee for my advice. I could charge them an hourly rate, like a consultant. Or, I could charge, say, 1% of whatever my clients' assets are worth at the end of the year, based on my recommendations or money management services.

This all describes the player known as an **investment adviser**. An investment adviser is a firm or a sole practitioner that charges folks for advice, rather than buying and selling securities. The folks who work for the investment adviser are called **investment adviser** *representatives*.

Huge difference between the two.

Just like with agents and broker-dealers, remember:

AN INVESTMENT ADVISER IS NEVER AN INVESTMENT ADVISER REPRESENTATIVE, AND AN INVESTMENT ADVISER REPRESENTATIVE IS NEVER AN INVESTMENT ADVISER.

One is the firm (investment adviser). The other is the individual who works for the firm (investment adviser representative). Sammy Sosa plays for the Cubs; Sammy Sosa is NOT the Cubs.

In other words, somebody gets her Series 65 license, allowing her to do "fee-based money management." Well, she probably doesn't want to meet the minimum net capital requirement of an advisory firm, so she goes to work for a firm rather than trying to fly solo. In other words, she represents an investment adviser, which is why they call folks like her investment adviser *representatives*. If she helps to make recommendations to clients or smiles and dials to set up appointments for the firm, she has to register as an investment adviser representative. Or, if she supervises people who do that kind of stuff, she has to be a registered investment adviser representative. The employees performing clerical/ministerial work are not defined as "investment adviser representatives." **But, if the employee is managing accounts, determining recommendations, making recommendations, or selling the services of the firm—now that person is an investment adviser representative and must register.**

So, one business helps folks buy and sell securities, either as brokers or as dealers. Those firms are called broker-dealers. The individuals who work for the broker-dealers pitching securities are called agents or registered representatives.

Another type of business doesn't sell securities; they sell advice and money management services. These firms are called investment advisers. And the folks who represent the investment advisers are called investment adviser representatives.

Here is the verbatim, legalistic definition of "investment adviser":

"Investment adviser" means any person who, for compensation, engages in the business of advising others, either directly or through publications or writings, as to the value of securities or as to the advisability of investing in, purchasing, or selling securities, or who, for compensation and as part of a regular business, issues or promulgates analyses or reports concerning securities; **but does not include (A)** a bank, or any bank holding company as defined in the Bank Holding Company Act of 1956, which is not an investment company, except that the term "investment adviser" includes any bank or bank holding company to the extent that such bank or bank holding company serves or acts as an investment adviser to a registered investment company, but if, in the case of a bank, such services or actions are performed through a separately identifiable department or division, the department or division, and not the bank itself, shall be deemed to be the investment adviser; **(B)** any lawyer, accountant, engineer, or teacher whose performance of such services is solely incidental to the practice of his profession; **(C)** any broker or dealer whose performance of such services is solely incidental to the conduct of his business as a broker or dealer and who receives no special compensation therefor; **(D)** the publisher of any bona fide newspaper, news magazine or business or financial publication of general and regular circulation; **(E)** any person whose advice, analyses, or reports relate to no securities other than securities which are direct obligations of or obligations guaranteed as to principal or interest by the United States, or securities issued or guaranteed by corporations in which the United States has a direct or indirect interest which shall have been designated by the Secretary of the Treasury, pursuant to section 3(a)(12) of the Securities Exchange Act of 1934, as exempted securities for the purposes of that Act; or **(F)** such other persons not within the intent of this paragraph, as the Commission may designate by rules and regulations or order.

Aren't you glad I'm not communicating to you solely in legalese, as my so-called "competitors" like to do? See, that makes *their* job a lot easier. All they have to do is cut and paste sections of the law and throw it in your face, leaving you with all the hard work and frustration. I figure you pay good money for this material, so I'll go ahead and do some of the hard work for you.

A radical concept.

Anyway, we've already seen that many folks who look like agents or broker-dealers have all kinds of excuses as to why they aren't, in fact, either, right? Well, plenty of folks who look like investment advisers actually turn out *not* to be by definition, which saves them all kinds of time, money, and aggravation. First of all, everybody has an opinion about securities. Not everybody is an investment adviser. I can stand on a street corner shouting for folks to buy convertible debentures in counter-cyclical issues whenever the yield curve inverts, but that wouldn't make me an investment adviser. Just one of the least understood street preachers in America. Unless I started charging for my advice, nobody would hassle me or try to define me as an investment adviser.

Broker-dealers and agents have all kinds of opinions about securities. As long as they don't charge a fee for the opinion, they aren't defined as investment advisers. Banks, savings & loans, and trust companies are never investment advisers but are defined, rather, as banks, savings & loans, and trust companies, respectively. If they want to get into the managed funds business, they have to set up a separate entity and register it as an investment adviser, just as they have to do if they want to set up a broker-dealership.

The Wall Street Journal passes out all kinds of advice in exchange for the subscription or newsstand price. That doesn't make them an investment adviser. You'd have to be rendering specific advice based on a specific situation and charging a fee for it before anyone would accuse you of being an investment adviser.

Lawyers, accountants, teachers, and engineers could all, theoretically, end up giving advice about a particular security to a particular client. Lawyers could be doing estate planning. An accountant could be advising somebody to do some tax-loss selling. A teacher could be teaching about the value of IBM stock. And a structural engineer could be rendering his opinion that a bridge built from the proceeds of a revenue bond is structurally sound. In none of those cases is the professional acting as an investment adviser. Remember the acronym LATE. Lawyers, accountants, teachers, and engineers who give incidental advice without charging a separate fee are not investment advisers.

Doesn't mean they're *never* investment advisers. If they hold themselves out to the public as being in the business of providing specific advice as to the value of securities, then they are an adviser and would have to register. But if the advice is incidental to their practice, and they don't charge a fee for the advice, they're excluded from the definition. Also note that geologists and geophysicists can also be granted the same exemption given to engineers.

If the firm only advises insurance companies it is exempt from registration with both the state and the feds (SEC). And, as you may (or may not) have read in the preceding legalistic ramble under point (E), if the advice only pertains to direct US Gov't obligations (Treasuries, GNMA, STRIPS, etc.), then the IA is excluded from the definition of IA and would not have to register.

If the term "investment adviser" applies to a firm, that means the firm is defined as such at the state level, giving the state jurisdiction/authority over that firm. But many firms are covered at the federal level, and guess what we call them?

Federal covered.

Just means the SEC is watching them, the lucky devils. A federal covered adviser is, therefore, not defined as an investment adviser at the state level. It's defined as an investment adviser at the federal level. Federal covered.

If the firm manages $25 million or more in assets, it has to register with the SEC and is, therefore, a federal covered adviser. If the firm manages less than $25 million, the firm registers at the state level.

Also, if the firm advises registered investment companies, they are federal covered. Federal covered advisers are <u>covered</u> at the <u>federal</u> level. They still provide the state with some professional courtesies in the form of paying their fees, filing a *consent to service of process*, and giving them the same paperwork they filed with the SEC.

But really they're on the SEC's turf, whereas a mere "investment adviser" is on the turf of the state securities Administrator.

Now it's getting interesting, huh!

Just like with broker-dealers, if the adviser has an office in the state, they have to register, unless granted some exemption. But if they *don't* have an office in the state, they usually don't have to register. The Administrator checks to see whom the out-of-state adviser is doing business with. If it's those big, multimillion-dollar institutions (insurance, bank, pension, mutual fund), then, we won't even define the firm as an "investment adviser." They can deal with as many of the big guys as they want. We'll even let them deal with exactly 5 little guys in the state without getting all bent out of shape about it. But if the adviser has more than 5 non-institutional clients in a 12-month period, that adviser will have to register in our state. The "under 6 little guys" rule is known as the *de minimus exemption*, which means, as you may recall, "so few it really don't matter" in the original Latin.

Investment advisers—firms—can be federal covered. Investment adviser representatives are NOT federal covered. If they have an office in the state, they have to register in the state, end of story.

Fascinating stuff, isn't it?

And here is the legalistic version:

Investment Adviser does NOT include:

- Investment adviser representative

- Bank, savings institution, or trust company

- Broker-dealer or its agent with incidental advisory services for no special compensation

- Lawyer, accountant, teacher, engineer, with advisory services incidental to (not integral component of) the practice

- Publisher of a newspaper or column which does not render advice on specific investment situation of each client

- Federal covered adviser

- Others as Administrator may by rule or order designate

Anyway, let's take some practice swings at defining who is and isn't an "investment adviser" or "investment adviser representative."

17. Which two of the following would be defined as investment advisers under the USA?

    I.   an economics professor with an active consulting business providing regular advice to pension funds as to which money managers to retain for the fund

    II.   a federal or state-charted bank

    III. a property & casualty insurance company

    IV. a lawyer who frequently advises non-accredited investors as to the value or advisability of investing in particular securities

    A.   I, II

    B.   I, IV

    C.   II, III

    D.   II, IV

18. All of the following persons are investment adviser representatives except

    A.   individual employed by a federal covered adviser who determines recommendations for clients

    B.   individual selling the advisory services of a federal covered adviser

    C.   individual performing clerical work for an investment adviser

    D.   person supervising those who sell the services of an advisory firm

19. A federal covered adviser must do all of the following except

    A.   pay fees to the state

    B.   submit a consent to service of process

    C.   provide notice to the state

    D.   submit to surprise inspections by the Administrator

20. Which of the following persons are defined as investment advisers under USA?

    A.   an investment adviser representative who helps determine client recommendations

    B.   a lawyer who occasionally provides advice as to the specific value of securities and charges a separate fee

    C.   a federal covered adviser

    D.   none of the above

21. Which of the following persons would have to register in the state of Mississippi?

    A.   an investment adviser representative with an office in the state of Mississippi working for a federal covered adviser located in Mississippi

    B.   an investment adviser properly registered in Utah who sends faxes and emails to 6 individuals residing in Mississippi

    C.   an investment adviser properly registered in Mississippi who provides specific advice as to the value of securities to 12 banks located in Mississippi.

    D.   all of the above

IA's and IA Reps—Fraud and Other Prohibited Activities

Now that we know who is and isn't an adviser or an adviser representative, let's talk about what these folks can and can not do.

As the USA states:

Section 102. [Advisory Activities]

    (a)   It is unlawful for any person who receives any consideration from another person primarily for advising the other person as to the value of securities or their purchase or sale, whether through the issuance of analyses or reports or otherwise,

    (1)   to employ any device, scheme, or artifice to defraud the other person, or

    (2)   to engage in any act, practice, or course of business which operates or would operate as a fraud or deceit upon the other person.

Fraud

So, if you as an individual (sole proprietor) or an advisory firm (partnership, corporation) get compensation for providing advice as to the value of securities or the advisability of their purchase or sale, you had better not say or do anything that operates as a fraud or deceit.

Unless you want to face the proverbial 3 years and five grand penalty.

Not too surprising that the Administrator gets just as uptight about people selling investment advice as he/she does when people are selling securities in the state. Any deceit or fraud takes place, and the Administrator is going to come down hard. Even if it's a big or "federal covered" firm, the Administrator can make life real difficult for that firm. Remember, the Administrator might not have jurisdiction over a federal covered security or federal covered adviser in terms of filing and inspection requirements. But, anybody who commits fraud in the state—absolutely anybody—is subject to the Administrator's jurisdiction. NSMIA made it clear that certain securities and firms would register at the federal level and sort of get a hall pass at the state level, but it still reminded everyone that the Administrator is definitely the appropriate person to enforce anti-fraud rules in the state.

So, as always, fraud is bad.

However, if the adviser is <u>not</u> providing their expert advice at the time, they can lie all they want about things not related to the customer's securities/investment strategy. On their day off an adviser can tell some guy at the corner tavern that the Chicago White Sox have won more games over the past 75 years than any other team in the major leagues. Obviously, that would be a lie of disturbing proportions, but it has nothing to do with providing investment advice. An investment adviser, then, can NOT commit fraud when NOT providing advice to someone for a fee.

Not that you thought they could, but just in case you got that idea, remember:

AN INVESTMENT ADVISER CAN NOT COMMIT FRAUD WHEN NOT PROVIDING ADVICE

If we didn't have that rule, then ticked-off customers could come after their advisers if the firm said it was 50 degrees and rainy, when, in fact, the weather was 62 degrees and mostly sunny.

The USA states:

> (b) It is unlawful for any investment adviser to enter into, extend, or renew any investment advisory contract unless it provides in writing
>   (1)   that the investment adviser shall not be compensated on the basis of a share of capital gains upon or capital appreciation of the funds or any portion of the funds of the client;

It actually goes on a ways from there, but let's take a second to translate that back to English.

Advisory contracts must be in written form. All contracts between investment advisers and clients must be in writing. All terms of the contract must be disclosed: fees, services provided, termination procedure, etc. Investment advisers get paid a flat fee. They either charge hourly for their advice, or they manage a client's money, taking a flat percentage of the assets over time. Maybe they charge 1% of the assets. That's a great motivator for the adviser, right? One per cent of $150,000 is nice, but one per cent of $200,000 is even nicer. So, the percentage stays flat and the adviser's compensation only grows if the customer's assets grow.

Sounds like a great way to compensate an investment adviser, right?

Well, some folks would rather just give the adviser a share of the gains. Every time the adviser buys at 10 and sells at 18, the adviser gets a piece of that capital gain. What about the rest of the stocks, which all might be heading down the drain?

Who cares, right? We had one big gain, and I, as your adviser, demand my cut. Them other stocks simply didn't work out the way we figured—sorry about that.

Does that sound like a good way to compensate your adviser?

Probably not. If a client were to pay an adviser with a share of capital gains, the adviser could just focus on a few winners and let the rest of the stocks wither on the vine to the customer's great detriment.

That's why advisers shall NOT be compensated as a share of capital gains, but as a percentage of total assets under management over a specified period of time. And the contract has to state that, too. Big institutional investors might be able to compensate advisers for performance/capital gains/capital appreciation, but I don't think the Series 63 will go there. If it does, tell it that "sophisticated investors" can do that, or folks with $1.5 million net worth or $750,000 under management.

. . . . . .
(2)   that no assignment of the contract may be made by the investment adviser without the consent of the other party to the contract; and
(3)   that the investment adviser, if a partnership, shall notify the other party to the contract of any change in the membership of the partnership within a reasonable time after the change

No assignment of contract without client consent. Wouldn't you be ticked if you called up your advisory firm and found out that some new adviser rep you didn't know was now handling your account? That's why the account can only be passed off or "assigned" to another party with the written consent of the client.

Notification of change in partnership structure. If the advisory firm is organized as a partnership, whenever one of the partners withdraws or dies, or a new member is admitted, the firm must inform all clients in a reasonable time frame that the partnership structure has changed. Doesn't matter in this case if the change was due to a partner with a majority or minority interest. And—not that you thought otherwise—but if a minority partner is admitted, withdraws, or dies, that is not considered "assignment of contract."

Whew! Good thing you know that, huh?

And, just in case you feel cheated by not seeing the original, the USA clearly states:

. . . but, if the investment adviser is a partnership, no assignment of an investment advisory contract is considered to result from the death or withdrawal of a minority of the members of the investment adviser having only a minority interest in the business of the investment adviser, or from the admission to the investment adviser of one or more members who, after admission, will be only a minority of the members and will have only a minority interest in the business.

Perhaps I should spare you the original legalese from now on?

Unlawful for investment adviser to act as principal for own account without disclosing capacity and obtaining client's consent. Investment advisers and investment adviser representatives are often trying to convince their clients that they should buy a particular security. What if your adviser were telling you to buy 10,000 shares of some funky Bulletin Board stock for the past three weeks, and you then discovered he just happened to have purchased 10,000 shares of it himself recently and was desperate to unload them on somebody? Sounds like a conflict of interest, right? Well, that's why the adviser would have to disclose the fact that he/they will act as a principal in the transaction and get your written consent before doing the deal. To act as a principal just means the adviser will either buy the security for inventory from the customer or sell it out of inventory to the customer. It's okay to do it, as long as the potential conflict of interest is disclosed and the customer's written consent is given before the deal.

CUSTODY OF CLIENT FUNDS/SECURITIES.

Some advisers just give advice and leave it up to the client to act upon it. Other advisers actually take custody of the customer's money and securities and take discretion over the account. Well, if they're going to take that much control of the client's account, the adviser first has to check with the state securities Administrator to see if there is a rule prohibiting custody of client funds. If there's no rule against it, the adviser can take custody so long as they notify the Administrator in writing. Also note that if the adviser has discretion *or* custody, they will probably have to post a surety bond, depending on their net capital. For that matter, so will broker-dealers who have custody or discretion over client accounts.

If an advisory firm is trying to land new clients, it would probably be really tempting to show prospects what the firm has done for existing clients, disclosing the identity, affairs, or investments of their clients, especially the rich and famous ones.

Yeah, well the existing clients—as well as the Administrator—would probably have a problem with that. The only way the firm can **disclose the affairs of its clients** is if the clients give permission, or if the firm is forced to turn over the information by court order/subpoena, that sort of thing.

REQUIRED DISCLOSURES

When trying to land new accounts, firms would probably rather not have to disclose the fact that their liabilities are starting to exceed their assets; unfortunately, they have to disclose that fact. If the adviser has ever been hit with a legal or regulatory action material to the evaluation of the integrity/ability of the firm to do a good job for the potential customer, that has to be disclosed. And, if the adviser has been convicted of a securities-related violation in the past 10 years, the firm has to disclose that annoying fact within 48 hours of entering into the contract, or at the time of signing if the customer has 5 days to cancel. Not sure how the heck the firm will get the customer to sign on the dotted line after making such disclosures, but that's their problem. Shouldn't have gotten trouble in the first place, right?

Now see if you can get the same idea from the original legalese:

It is unlawful for any person advising another person for compensation as to the value of securities to:
- Employ any device, scheme, or artifice to defraud
- Engage in any act, practice, or course of business which operates as a fraud or deceit upon another person
- Knowingly act as a principal for his/their own account to sell or purchase any security from a client without disclosing in writing the capacity in which acting and obtaining client's consent
- Unlawful to enter into or renew advisory contract unless it provides that:
  - Adviser shall not be compensated on basis of share of capital gains
  - Adviser can be compensated on basis of total value of funds under management over a specified period of time
- No assignment of contract without consent of client
  - If partnership, death, withdrawal, or admission of members having minority interest is not considered assignment
  - Adviser, if partnership, shall notify clients of any change in membership of partnership within reasonable time
- Advisor may not take custody if Administrator prohibits custody, or, in absence of rule, adviser fails to notify the Administrator

Anyway, let's do some questions on prohibited/unethical practices by investment advisers and investment adviser representatives.

22. **Which of the following activities is/are not prohibited?**
    A.   an investment adviser representative tells a prospective client that she has been certified by the state Administrator
    B.   an investment adviser gains new clients by showing prospects what he has done specifically for his other customers' accounts
    C.   in the absence of a rule, an advisory firm takes custody of client funds and then notifies the Administrator in writing
    D.   all of the above

23. **All of the following activities are prohibited except:**
    A.   omitting an immaterial statement to avoid confusing a client about to make a suitable investment
    B.   an advisory client's assets fall below a minimum level, and the firm transfers the account to an office in another state
    C.   an investment adviser representative recommends that clients make purchases based on material inside information
    D.   an investment adviser representative recommends municipal securities to all clients of the firm without investigating the clients' financial backgrounds

24. **Which of the following statements is true concerning investment advisers with custody of client securities and/or funds?**
    A.   this practice is illegal in all cases
    B.   the adviser must send to clients monthly an itemized statement showing the funds and securities in the adviser's custody and all debits, credits, and transactions over such period
    C.   at least once per year the adviser must schedule an inspection by a CPA or public accountant, who will file a statement with the Administrator promptly afterward
    D.   unless the Administrator specifically prohibits custody of client funds/securities, the adviser may take custody of client funds/securities if written notice is sent to the Administrator

25. **All of the following activities by an investment adviser are prohibited except**
    A.   entering into a contract that clearly states compensation shall be a percentage of capital gains
    B.   entering into a verbal contract with a client
    C.   entering into a contract with a customer that clearly discloses services, terms, fees, whether discretionary or non-discretionary, and the fact that no assignment of contract is allowed without written client consent
    D.   disclosing the identity, affairs or investments of a client to a third party without consent of client or court order

Registration of Persons: Agents, Broker-Dealers, IA's, IA Reps

So we've defined who is and is not considered an agent, broker-dealer, investment adviser and investment adviser representative. We've discussed what these "persons" (legal entities) can and can not do.

Now let's talk about what they have to do in order to register and keep their registration effective at the state level.

The USA clearly states, "It is unlawful for any person to transact business in this state as a broker-dealer or agent unless he is registered under this act (or excluded/ exempted from registration)." And, "It is unlawful for any broker-dealer or issuer to employ an agent unless the agent is registered. The registration of an agent is not effective during any period when he is not associated with a particular broker-dealer registered under this act or a particular issuer." That means **NO PARKING**. As the USA clearly indicates, if you are not associated with a particular broker-dealer or issuer, your registration as an agent is not effective. Also note that if your broker-dealer employer loses their license, your license as an agent is no good, either.

"When an agent begins or terminates a connection with a broker-dealer or issuer, or begins or terminates those activities which make him an agent, the agent as well as the broker-dealer or issuer shall promptly notify the Administrator." So, if you get a question about who must notify the Administrator when an agent leaves one broker-dealer to go work for another broker-dealer, remember it's all three: both firms plus the agent.

Section 202 of the USA states that, "A broker-dealer, agent, or investment adviser may obtain an initial or renewal registration by filing with the Administrator an application together with a **consent to service of process**." The law even uses surprising language such as, "Every application for registration under this act and every issuer which proposes to offer a security in this state . . . shall file with the Administrator . . . an irrevocable **consent** appointing the Administrator to be his attorney to receive service of any lawful process in any non-criminal suit, action, or proceeding against him . . . with the same force and validity as if served personally on the person filing the consent." So, a **consent to service of process** is a form that gives the Administrator the power to receive court papers on the registrant's behalf, should the registrant get into hot water. In other words, you file this consent to service of process so that if you screw up and flee the state, the other party can still nail you with court papers by serving them on the Administrator and sending a copy to you at your latest known address.

So, what has to be provided to the Administrator in the application?

You guessed it—that's entirely up to the Administrator. As Section 202 states:

> The application shall contain whatever information the Administrator by rule requires concerning such matters as:
> - the applicant's form and place of organization
> - the applicant's proposed method of doing business
> - the qualifications and business history of the applicant; in the case of a broker-dealer or investment adviser, the qualifications and business history of any partner, officer, or director
> - (4) any injunction or administrative order or conviction of a misdemeanor involving a security or any aspect of the securities business and any conviction of a felony; and
> - (5) the applicant's financial condition and history.

The Administrator can also make someone filing an initial application publish an announcement in one or more specified newspapers published in the state. Just like when you start a business of any kind, you publish a notification in a newspaper, right? And, when does the registration become effective? As long as no denial order is in effect and no proceeding is pending (denial, revocation, suspension), the registration becomes effective at noon of the 30th day after an application is filed. The Administrator can also make the application effective earlier than the 30th day, and if any amendments are filed to the application, the Administrator can defer the effectiveness until the 30th day after filing the amendment.

So, it's 30 days, basically, unless the Administrator makes it effective earlier.

And, not surprisingly, when you file an application, you also must **pay fees** to the state. The exact amount is up to each Administrator.

You might get a question about a "successor firm." Just remember that a broker-dealer or investment adviser may file an application for registration of a successor firm, whether or not the successor firm is then in existence, for the unexpired portion of the year. And, there is no fee to pay in that case—remember there is an "unexpired portion" left on the registration. So, if your broker-dealer was a partnership that is now going to become a corporation, you may register the new entity for the remaining portion of your existing registration without paying a fee . . . even if the new firm is not yet in existence.

If an agent has discretion over a client's account, the agent may be forced to post a surety/fidelity bond to protect against theft/embezzlement. This can be satisfied by posting the bond or depositing cash and/or securities.

That is not a "minimum net capital" requirement, though. Firms have minimum net capital requirements, and—as we may have pointed out before—an agent is not a broker-dealer and an investment adviser representative is not an investment adviser.

Firms have minimum net capital requirements, not individuals. The USA states, "The Administrator may by rule require a minimum capital for registered broker-dealers and investment advisers." NASAA's "Investment Adviser Net Worth/Bonding Rule," states that an adviser with custody of client funds or securities must at all times maintain a net worth of $35,000. An adviser without custody, but who has discretion (power to choose) over a client's account must maintain at all times a minimum net worth of $10,000. So, there's a higher standard for advisers who have possession of the client's funds/securities than for those who are allowed to choose the Asset/Activity/Amount on any transaction. An Adviser who accepts prepayment of $500 or more 6 or more months in advance must at all times maintain positive net worth, too. Remember that the states can never impose a higher standard here than imposed by the federal regulators under the Securities Exchange Act of 1934.

If the firm does not have the required minimum net worth (assets minus liabilities), the firm must post a bond in an amount determined by the Administrator based on the number of clients and the total assets under management. The bonds will be in the amount of the net worth deficiency/shortfall rounded up to the nearest $5,000. Rather than post a bond, the firm can also just deposit either cash or securities, and the Act says the Administrator can not force the firm to deposit cash—the Administrator must accept a deposit of securities, usually Treasury securities rather than, say, E-toys.

Things change in the securities business, so if the firm's net worth falls below the minimum requirement, the firm must notify the Administrator of the shortfall by the close of business on the next business day. And by the close of business of the next business day following this notification, the firm must file a report with the Administrator of its financial condition. So on Monday at 11 o'clock A.M. your advisory firm realizes their net worth is deficient. By the close of business on Tuesday they must notify the Administrator. And by the close of business on Wednesday, they must file an updated statement of financial condition.

The USA states, "Every registered broker-dealer and investment adviser shall make and keep such accounts, correspondence, memoranda, papers, books, and other records as the Administrator by rule prescribes. All records so required shall be preserved for three years unless the Administrator by rule prescribes otherwise for particular types of records."

But remember that investment advisers actually keep their records for five years now, due to a relatively recent update.

So, if the test question asks about a broker-dealer, tell it three years. If it's about an IA—five years.

And then move on with your life.

The Act also goes on to point out that every investment adviser and broker-dealer must file financial reports as required by the Administrator. The Administrator has the power to determine which reports must be filed, what the contents of those reports are, and when they have to be certified by independent or certified public accountants. Financial reports are to be prepared in accordance with Generally Accepted Accounting Principles (GAAP). If any information in any of the documents filed with the Administrator becomes inaccurate or incomplete in any material respect, the Administrator must be informed promptly. And—guess what—the Administrator may send somebody to your advisory firm or broker-dealer who would like to have a little look-see at all your records. Heck, if he/she isn't too busy, the Administrator might even drop by him or herself.

Surprise! We're here! Sure hope all your files are in order.

This power to inspect is called "visitatorial power," and they don't need a subpoena to get you to, like, open the door for them. If you refuse to allow the inspection, right there you have violated the Act. And that could lead to an injunction, a revocation, or even a criminal prosecution, which is bad. The Administrator can even make firms foot the bill for the expense of performing these inspections, which isn't that surprising, really, given your understanding of the Act at this point.

Persons and securities that must register at the state level are subject to the Administrator's power to deny, revoke, or suspend a registration. **Denial, revocation,** and **suspension** imply that somebody has done somebody wrong. The Administrator, remember, is out to protect the average investor, so if it is "in the public interest," meaning it provides needed protection for investors, the Administrator can prevent a security from being offered or a person from setting up shop (deny). Or, the Administrator can make a security's underwriters—or tell an agent—to take a time out (suspend). Or, the Administrator can even take back a security's registration or the license of a broker-dealer (revoke).

Usually, you'd have to do something pretty bad, like lie, cheat or steal for any of that bad stuff to happen. But an agent, broker-dealer, or investment adviser's registration could certainly end up being denied, suspended, or revoked if the Administrator feels it is in the public interest <u>and the person</u>:

—has filed an application for registration which as of its effective date, or as of any date after filing in the case of an order denying effectiveness, was incomplete in any material respect or contained any statement which was, in light of the circumstances under which it was made, false or misleading with respect to any material fact

—has willfully violated or willfully failed to comply with any provision of this act or a predecessor act or any rule or order under this act or a predecessor act

—was convicted within last 10 years of any <u>securities-related</u> misdemeanor or *any* felony

—is/has been enjoined by any court from engaging in securities business, or been subject to adjudication within past 10 years under federal securities laws

—has engaged in dishonest or unethical practices in the securities business

So, if a registered rep files a registration with the Administrator, the Administrator can always **deny** the registration if he discovers that the rep was convicted of knocking off liquor stores 7 years ago, or selling unregistered non-exempt securities within 10 years. Any felony can get the rep in trouble, but a misdemeanor has to be related to money and/or securities. If the rep has been working a few years before the Administrator discovers that the rep filed a false or incomplete application—seems he somehow forgot to mention that little incident as a bank teller—the Administrator can **suspend** or even **revoke** the registration. Notice how they made the law nice and vague by using language such as "has engaged in dishonest or unethical practices in the securities business."

Pretty broad, huh? And guess who determines if something is dishonest or unethical?

The Administrator.

You can appeal his/her order to deny, suspend, or revoke, but now you're talking about missing work, paying legal fees, and generally having not too many good days for a while.

In any case, something bad has happened causing the Administrator to deny, suspend, or revoke an application/registration. Other situations that could lead to a denial, suspension or revocation include:

—The person (rep, firm) is insolvent
  • for firms, a formal finding of insolvency is required
  • for individuals, as soon as liabilities exceed assets, they're toast

How would you like to have a registered rep handling your account when the rep is about to go bankrupt? Gee, that might explain all those hard-charging phone calls you've been getting from him, huh? That's why the Administrator can suspend or revoke the rep's license as soon as his liabilities exceed his assets. If it's a firm that's sailing into troubled financial waters, a formal finding of insolvency would be required, as in bring in the auditors—these numbers don't quite add up here.

> —The person isn't qualified because they lack training, experience, *and* knowledge
> • lack of experience isn't enough all by itself if the applicant does have training and knowledge

Lack of experience isn't a good enough reason all by itself, but if the representative has no training, no knowledge, AND no experience, the Administrator could deny the registration. But lack of experience would not be a fair reason all by itself, since the only way for someone to gain experience is to be allowed to gain some experience. Right?

If the person has been enjoined by any court from engaging in the securities business, or has been subject to adjudication within the past 10 years under federal securities laws, the registration can be denied, revoked, or suspended. That's just fancy language for saying that if a court has slapped an injunction on the person in the past 10 years due to anything even remotely related to securities, that person is toast.

Also if the applicant/registrant:
- Has failed reasonably to supervise his agents if he is a broker-dealer or his employees if he is an investment adviser
- Has failed to pay the proper filing fee; but the Administrator may enter only a denial order under this clause, and shall vacate any such order when the deficiency has been corrected.

So, if a broker-dealer or investment adviser is trying to get registered, they could be denied if they've shown a history of failing to supervise their representatives. And, if the registrant hasn't paid proper filing fees, the registration for a security or license could be denied until the fees are paid—but the order would be vacated as soon as the fees were paid up.

Pay the state. It's easier that way.

Many broker-dealers are also investment advisers. However, if the firm tries to register or renew a registration and the Administrator is convinced they have no business being in business as an investment adviser, he can condition the granting of their broker-dealer license on their *not* acting as an investment adviser.

Hmm, just when you thought this stuff was starting to get a little dry, huh?

The law also says that the Administrator may not institute a suspension or revocation proceeding on the basis of a fact or transaction known to him when registration became effective unless the proceeding is instituted within the next thirty days. I am confident the exam will not ask you about that, unless it does. And, it's possible that the test will ask if the Administrator can make a rule that forces agents or broker-dealers or any class of applicants to take an exam, either oral or written. How would you answer that?

Yes. Remember, the Administrator can do all kinds of stuff. If you memorize the few things he *can't* do, you'll be fine. Can't issue an injunction; can't sentence folks to prison; can't issue the big orders (stop, deny, revoke, suspend) without prior notice, an opportunity for hearing, and written findings of fact and conclusions of law. But other than that . . .

Okay, now if the Administrator is going to step in and deny, suspend or revoke somebody's registration, that somebody has to be given prior notice, an opportunity for a hearing, and written findings of fact and conclusions of law. The hearing, by the way, has to be a public hearing, unless all parties agree to keep it behind closed doors.

But, if we're talking about a pending registration (hasn't even been granted yet), the Administrator can "summarily suspend" the registration, with or without prior notice and an opportunity for a public hearing. Maybe the Administrator has lunch with an old college buddy who says something about a broker-dealer who might have gotten into some trouble in the state of Mississippi a few years ago. If that broker-dealer has a pending registration with the Administrator, one which somehow failed to mention the Mississippi mishap, the Administrator can *summarily suspend* that pending registration until he's had a chance to look into the matter more thoroughly. The broker-dealer will be given an opportunity for a hearing, but that's <u>after</u> the order to summarily suspend has been entered. On the other hand, if we were talking about a denial, suspension, or revocation order, the broker-dealer would have to be given <u>prior notice</u> with an opportunity for a hearing and written findings of fact *before* the order is entered.

You also might see a test question similar to this:

Does the Administrator **cancel** a registration for the same reasons that he/they would deny, revoke, or suspend a registration?

The answer? No.

If a registration is **canceled**, that just means the party no longer exists. They've left the state, for example. If the office can't be located, or if the person has been declared mentally incompetent by a court of law, the Administrator can cancel the registration. In other words, if the party no longer appears to exist, either mentally or physically, the registration is canceled. Doesn't imply that somebody did anything wrong.

Finally, a withdrawal occurs when the person filing the registration changes his/ their mind. They decide, for example, that they aren't going to do any business in New Hampshire, so why go through the hassle of registering there? We'll just withdraw that one, no big deal.

When do registrations of persons expire?

On December 31st of each year, unless properly renewed.

26. **Criminal penalties under USA include which two of the following?**
    I.   five years in jail
    II.   three years in jail
    III. $5,000 fine
    IV. $3,000 fine
    A.   I, III
    B.   I, IV
    C.   II, III
    D.   II, IV

27. **Which of the following actions may the Administrator take without prior notice?**
    A.   issue an injunction
    B.   stop order
    C.   summary suspension of a pending registration
    D.   all of the above

28. **The Administrator has the authority to do all of the following except:**
    A.   publish violations in a newspaper and/or website
    B.   enforce subpoenas issued by Administrators of other states
    C.   investigate in other states
    D.   sentence violators to three years in prison

SECURITIES

If your money is secure, it's not a security. It's only a security if your money isn't secure.

Seriously.

If something has a fixed or guaranteed payment, that something is NOT a security. So, a fixed annuity is not a security.

A variable annuity, which exposes the investor to the ups and downs of the stock market, now *that's* a security, since the investor's money is no longer secure.

Precious metals, commodities . . . way too tangible to be securities. Corn is a commodity, it's a tangible thing. It is, therefore, not a security. If you own a cow, guess what you actually own?

A cow.

But if you sell somebody an ownership interest in your cattle, that ownership interest can be defined as a "security." A security is "paper tradable for value." So the option (put, call) on a corn futures (commodities) contract would be a security, because the option is paper tradable for value. The commodity itself (the corn sitting in a bushel) is not a security.

As determined by the "Howey Decision" a **security** is, basically, three things:

- an investment of money in a common enterprise
- money at risk
- investor hopes to gain through efforts of others

So, if there's no money at risk, it's not a security. Just remember what isn't a security, and you'll be fine.

You also will want to consult the long list of all the things that are securities.

A security is:

- note
- stock

- treasury stock
- bond
- debenture
- evidence of indebtedness
- certificate of interest or participation in any profit-sharing agreement
- collateral-trust certificate
- preorganization certificate or subscription
- transferable share
- <u>option</u> on commodity/futures contract
- investment contract
- voting-trust certificate
- certificate of deposit for a security
- certificate of interest or participation in an oil, gas, or mining title or lease or in payments out of production under such a title or lease
- in general, any interest or instrument commonly known as a "security"
- warrant, right, or option for a security
- variable annuity or variable life insurance policy
- whiskey warehouse receipts

A security does NOT include:
- fixed insurance or endowment policy
- term insurance policy
- fixed annuity, either lump sum or periodic
- futures contract
- precious metals

OFFERS AND SALES

An **offer** is an attempt to sell a security. A **sale** only takes place when something is actually transferred to somebody for value. *A contract to dispose of a security for value* would be a common way to define a sale.

Why does the law use such language?

By using language like "anything commonly known as a security," you're probably going to catch just about anything you want to regulate. You use phrases such as, "dispose of a security for value," rather than writing something precise like, "receiving money for a stock." If you did it the second, more precise, way, some weasel could break the law by either selling a *bond* (hey, a bond ain't a stock, and a stock ain't a bond) or rather than taking *money* accept a new Jaguar (hey, a car isn't money; and money isn't a car).

Nope. The folks who write rules and regulations can think of just about everything before they write the rules and regulations, and when things pop up later that expose weakness in the rules, they just re-convene and re-write the rules to catch the new stuff, too.

And then you get to sit for some complicated, bizarre test called the Series 63, but that's another matter.

Anyway, selling securities is an activity that is highly regulated and probably should be. The average Joe has little understanding of stocks, bonds, commercial paper, mutual funds, etc. So, the securities Administrator makes sure that agents, advisers, and broker-dealers do not take advantage of unskilled individual investors by violating basic rules designed to protect the average Joe and JoAnn from unscrupulous professionals.

The first thing these professionals can not do is lie to investors about **material facts**. A material fact is directly related to a particular security's value. If an unscrupulous registered rep knew that a particular company had missed its earnings projections three quarters in a row and told a customer that, in fact, the company "always made their numbers," that would be fraud—intentional deceit designed for financial gain. The Administrator doesn't put up with that nonsense and customers do, in fact, call the Administrator, especially if they end up losing money because of the lie.

Of course, an *immaterial* fact is *immaterial*, meaning it don't got nothin' to do with nothin'. So, if the lie had nothing to do with a material fact, that's a different matter. For example, the rep tells the customer that Ford is going to paint one of their visitor lobbies green, when the color turns out to be, in fact, chartreuse. Who cares, right? The color of the visitor lobby is *im*material to the decision of whether to purchase a stock or bond issued by the Ford Motor Company.

Whether the company is expected to meet its earnings projections, grow its market share, attract top management talent . . . those are all material to the future viability of the company and the health of its stock, right? In other words, that stuff is material to the investment decision. An agent not only can not lie about material facts; he or she also can not forget to tell a customer a material fact. Omitting material facts is a no-no, just like misstating material facts. Make sure the fact is *material*, though, before you make an answer choice.

Some securities are exempt from the filing requirements under the Securities Act of 1933. Government securities, munibonds, church bonds, etc. all have exemptions from the filing requirements. Those are called **exempt securities**. But if a security does not have an exemption, it is a **non-exempt security** that needs to be registered. So on the exam if you see somebody trying to sell non-exempt unregistered securities, sit up and take notice. This is a no-no of the highest order. Non-exempt, non-registered securities may not be offered or sold. They need to be registered because they have no exemption, right? Now, if somebody tries to sell an unregistered, *exempt* security, that's fine. If it's exempt, it doesn't have to be registered, anyway. But if it's non-exempt, it has to be registered before it can be offered or sold. So, if you've gone through the long list of possible exemptions—exempt issuer, exempt security, exempt transaction—and you just can't find an excuse/exemption, then those are the securities that have to be registered. The non-exempt ones.

So, all securities have to be registered, except the exempt ones.

If the security is exempt, it has an excuse from registration.

But, if there is no excuse/exemption, then the security does have to be registered.

Which means that non-exempt securities are really the ones that have to be registered.

Because they have no excuse. No exemption. Non-exempt.

29. **Which of the following are not securities?**
    A.   whiskey warehouse receipts
    B.   interests in multilevel distributorships
    C.   fixed annuities
    D.   all of the above

30. **In which of the following instances has an agent sold a security?**
    A.   a broker-dealer transfers a treasury note for value
    B.   an investment representative donates securities to a charitable organization
    C.   an investment representative sells a variable annuity to a high net worth client
    D.   all of the above

31. **An agent unknowingly sold an unregistered non-exempt security to a high net worth individual who could easily afford the risks involved. This action is**
    A.   prohibited and fraudulent under USA
    B.   not prohibited but fraudulent under USA
    C.   prohibited but not fraudulent for high net worth individuals
    D.   prohibited but not fraudulent under USA

32. **Which of the following are not prohibited practices?**
    A.   omitting an immaterial fact to avoid distracting a client who is thinking of a less suitable alternative
    B.   executing more than 100 transactions in a month for a high net worth client with a large appetite for risk
    C.   selling an unregistered exempt security not registered in the state in which the agent works
    D.   all of the above

33. **In which of the following cases has a sale of securities occurred?**
    A.   an agent transfers interests in farm animals for value
    B.   an agent sells 10 clients variable annuities to 10 clients
    C.   an agent sells 10 whiskey warehouse receipts to 10 clients
    D.   all of the above

Because of NSMIA (National Securities Markets Improvement Act) most issuers of securities register with the SEC and, therefore, do not have to register with the state Administrators. This prevents redundant registration processes and unnecessary red tape. Most securities, in fact, are "federal covered" and do not have to register at the state level. These include:

- any security traded on any recognized exchange or quoted on NASDAQ's National Market or Small Cap List
- investment company shares
- any security exempt from the Act of 1933 (govies, munis, church bonds, etc.)

So, if you're exempt from the Act of 1933, that means you're exempt at the federal level, so you really couldn't care less about the state level, either. And, if you've been defined as "federal covered" by NSMIA, you can just deal with the SEC and not worry about the state's requirements for filing. Listed and NASDAQ securities deal with the SEC, which is plenty to deal with as it turns out. The only thing required of these securities is a "notice filing," which is exactly what it sounds like. We're just notifying the Administrator that we'll be selling securities in his state. He doesn't have jurisdiction over us in the sense that we have to pass a "merit test," but—as always—if anybody commits fraud in the Administrator's state, he/she/they have the power to go after us. So we're filing a notice, a sort of official "heads up" that we'll be in the state raising money by selling securities that are either exempt at the federal level or covered specifically at the federal level.

But, if the security is Unlisted and *not* quoted on NASDAQ and NOT exempt (non-exempt) from the Act of 1933, it <u>will</u> have to be registered at the state level. So, it's the Bulletin Board and Pink Sheet stocks that have to worry about state-level registration. There are three methods of registering securities with the State Securities Administrator, although I would only expect you to see "coordination" and/or "qualification" on the exam.

Registration by **coordination** is the most common method for Initial Public Offerings (IPO's). As the name implies, the issuer *coordinates* the state-level registration with the federal (SEC) registration. In order to use this method, the issuer must have a registration statement filed with the SEC. Otherwise, what would they be "coordinating," right? The issuer files the same paperwork with the state Administrator that they filed with the big guys at the SEC, including copies of the prospectus, articles of incorporation, underwriter agreements, and a specimen of the security.

Registration by coordination is effective concurrently/simultaneously with the federal registration, provided that paperwork has been on file for 10 days. Be careful here, though. The test question might say something like, "Registration by coordination is effective 10 days after the effectiveness at the federal level."

Not. Nothing is effective a specific number of days *after* anything. The registration for the security is effective either concurrently with the federal or whenever the Administrator says so. The paperwork must be on file for 10 days, but as long as that requirement is met, the effectiveness coincides with the federal release.

If an issuer has already done their IPO and would now like to sell additional shares to the public, they will most likely use registration by **filing**. This is the most common method for additional offerings, called "subsequent primary distributions." In order to qualify for this method the issuer must have a registration statement filed with the SEC. If they've been in business for 25 months, they don't qualify, because they must have been in continuous operation for 36 consecutive calendar months. They also must not have failed to pay bond interest or a preferred dividend and their stock must be trading for at least $5 per share. The issuer files with the state the same paperwork they filed with the SEC, and as long as the paperwork has been on file for 5 days, the registration is effective concurrently or simultaneously with the federal registration. Again, watch out for a statement such as, "Registration by filing becomes effective 5 days after the effectiveness of the federal registration." That ain't right—it's effective concurrently with the federal, provided that the information has been on file for 5 days. Again, nothing is effective a certain number of days after anything else.

The least desirable method for filing securities is called registration by **qualification**. Here you're on the state Administrator's home court, and your securities will only be effective if and when the Administrator says so. There is no set time frame. The securities are effective "when so ordered by" the Administrator. The issuer has to file any paperwork the Administrator wants to see. Why does the Administrator have so much power under registration by qualification? Because the SEC isn't involved. If the issuer hasn't filed a registration statement with the SEC, the issuer has to file with the state. Remember that coordination and filing both require filing with the SEC. Well, if you don't file with the SEC and you have no exemption from the registration process, you'll have to file with the state Administrator. If an Alabama issuer is only going to sell securities to Alabama residents the issuer would only file with the state of Alabama. Or maybe they're ready to do a subsequent primary distribution but have only been in continuous operation for 27 months. That doesn't meet the requirements for registration by filing, so the issuer will have to register by qualification.

No matter which method the issuer uses (coordination, filing, qualification) these are the general provisions for registering securities at the state/Blue Sky level:

- a registration statement may be filed by the issuer, any other person on whose behalf the offering is to be made, or a registered broker-dealer
- every registration statement shall include:
    - a filing fee
    - amount of securities offered in their state
    - <u>names</u> of other states where securities will be offered (not total $ amount)
    - any adverse order, judgment, or decree entered by a court, the securities agency or Administrator in any state, or the Securities and Exchange Commission in connection with the offering.
- registrations are effective for one year
- securities offered by coordination or qualification may be require an escrow account whose proceeds are impounded by the Administrator and not released to the issuer/underwriters until they have raised the specified amount
- the securities registration statement must include a consent to service of process

Finally, those big, bad "federal covered" securities usually do what's called a **"notice filing,"** which is exactly what it sounds like. They're being kind enough to give the Administrator a heads-up. We're in your state selling securities that are far too big and complicated for an insignificant little state-level regulator like you to possibly handle. They might have to provide the same documents filed with the SEC, but, again, they're really on the federal turf, as opposed to the state turf.

34. Which of the following statements is/are true?
   A. registration by coordination is effective 10 days after federal registration declared effective
   B. registration by filing is effective 5 days after federal registration declared effective
   C. registration by qualification is the most common method of registering IPO's
   D. none of the above

35. Which of the following must all state securities registrations include?
   A. names of all states where security will be offered
   B. total dollar amount of securities offered in all states
   C. neither
   D. both

36. Which of the following securities would have to be registered by qualification?
   A. XXO Corporation will sell its securities only to residents of Wisconsin and, therefore, will not file a registration statement with the SEC
   B. ORO Corporation made its initial public offering two and a half years earlier and now wishes to sell additional stock to the general public
   C. XXY Corporation plans to make an initial public offering only in the state of Illinois
   D. all of the above

SCOPE OF THE ACT, ADMINISTRATOR'S POWERS

The Uniform Securities Act gives the Administrator the power to regulate "persons." Which of the following are **persons**?

- Cleveland, Ohio
- the United States Government
- the State of Missouri
- New York City

The answer?

All of them. They are all legal entities able to open an investment account; therefore, the USA refers to them all as **persons**.

Some guy riding the commuter train is an *individual*. He's probably a **person**, too, but the term *person* is much larger than that. A person could be an individual, but it could also be a firm, or a government. It's easier to remember what a person isn't. A person is not:

- dead
- mentally incompetent
- a minor

So, as long as they're not dead, crazy, or a child, they're a **person**. So if a definition uses the word "person," it could be referring to an individual, a firm, or basically any legal entity. An individual is just an example of a person—a broker-dealer, investment adviser, and an issuer are all persons, too.

Administrator

Guess what we call the official or agency designated by state legislature or governor to ADMINISTER the securities laws of the state?

Yep, the **ADMINISTRATOR**.

How much power does the state securities Administrator have?

A lot.

The securities Administrator of the state of Illinois can actually investigate fraud both inside and outside the state of Illinois. Also, if he/they receive a subpoena from the Administrator of Wyoming, they can enforce it there in Illinois, too. In other words, crossing a state border will not shield anyone from the consequences of violating the securities laws of a state.

The Administrator loves to publish the names of folks who violate the state's securities laws, like a teacher writing the names of unruly children on the chalkboard. So if you get caught churning an account, borrowing from a customer, or making unsuitable recommendations, maybe you'll see your name in the papers or up on a website with a searchable database that all future employers can check.

So, the Administrator has a lot of power. However, the securities Administrator is not a court of law, so he/they can not sentence violators to prison or issue judicial injunctions—only courts can do that. But, they probably have some influence over getting somebody sent to prison or slapped with a judicial injunction, right? Administrators can make you come into their office, raise your right hand, swear to tell the truth, the whole truth, etc. Even if you've invoked your privileges under the Fifth Amendment, the Administrator can make you come in and give a statement under oath, anyway. Nothing you say can be used to incriminate you, but if the Administrator thinks you have something relevant to say, you'll have to talk to him/them at your earliest convenience.

If you commit a prohibited practice, like churning or making unsuitable recommendations, the Administrator can suspend or revoke your license. You have the right to receive prior notice and an opportunity for a hearing (except for summary suspension of a pending registration), but if the Administrator hears your side of the story and isn't impressed, your license can be denied, revoked, or suspended, which is bad. The hearing has to be a public hearing except in rare cases, and you can appeal the decision arrived at through the hearing to a court within 60 days, but that doesn't sound like much fun, right? Sounds like the Administrator has lots of power, right?

The exam kinda' wants to make that impression on you.

If you don't obey the Administrator's instructions, he will spew big ten-dollar words at you, like "contumacy," which means "failure to comply with an Administrator's order." **Contumacy**. If you commit the dreaded act of contumacy, the Administrator can go to the proper court of law and ask it to issue an order against your insubordinate little attitude, and neither the court nor the Administrator will be in a good mood next time they see you. If you fail to recognize the court's authority, now you're talking about **contempt** of court, which is *really* bad.

The Administrator can deny or suspend your license, but the Administrator turns criminal violations over to the courts. If somebody violates the state's securities laws, a court of law can fine them up to $5,000 and/or stick them in jail for up to three years, which is bad.

Three years, five grand. Memorize that. Those are the criminal penalties for violations of the Uniform Securities Act. If something is alleged to have happened more than five years ago, though, guess what? It's too late for anything to be done about it, since the statute of limitations has now expired. And, if a person can prove that they had no knowledge of a particular order they ended up violating, that person can not be put in prison. In other words, this is one case where ignorance of the law *is* an excuse. Of course, the burden of proof is on the person claiming ignorance, and who wants to be that guy?

The Administrator can issue a *cease and desist* order. This is basically an official warning that the regulators know what you did and ain't too thrilled about it. You now have a regulatory order issued against you, which you'll have to disclose to clients before somehow getting them to sign on the dotted line anyway. And, if you keep it up, you'll most likely end up having your license suspended or denied, which is bad. Now, you've got even more stuff to disclose to future clients, presuming against all odds that any other state would let you set up shop. The USA also says the Administrator can issue a "cease and desist" even in anticipation of a violation, which is like a time-out for a registered rep or a firm. It looks like they might be doing something wrong, so the Administrator issues a cease and desist order to make them stop what they're doing while he takes a closer look at the matter. Sort of like the principal at an elementary school taking a kid aside and saying, "Sorry, Johnny, I'm afraid I'm going to have to give you a time-out because I think it's likely you might smack somebody today after school. It's not a detention, mind you, just a time out to protect one of my kids from getting hurt by a little thug like you."

Cease and desist.

A *stop order* is a formal order stopping somebody from doing something permanently, or possibly stopping them from operating as a broker-dealer in the state. Basically, it's the category under which the words *deny*, *suspend*, and *revoke* belong. To deny/suspend/revoke basically means that the Administrator is "stop"-ping the security or person from doing what they were registered or are trying to get registered to do. To issue a "stop order," the Administrator has to give the party prior notice and an opportunity for a hearing.

So, if the exam got real funky on you and started babbling about cease & desist versus stop (which I highly doubt), just remember that a cease and desist can happen even without prior notice, while the more serious "stop" order requires prior written notice, et cetera.

The Administrator's orders can always be appealed to the appropriate court of law, but, not surprisingly, judicial reviews are final. The person affected has 60 days to file the appeal, by the way.

At what point does the Administrator's/USA's powers "kick in"?

Whenever an offer to sell is made in this state—meaning the offer either originated in the state or was directed into the state. So if an offer originates in the state of Washington and is directed into the state of Oregon, the Administrators of both states have authority should something funny take place. Remember, if an agent in Washington calls a customer who lives in Oregon trying to sell securities, an offer to sell securities has been made in both Washington and Oregon.

Which actually makes so much sense it's scary.

And if the customer drives to California before calling back to accept the offer to sell, now the state of California has power, too, because the offer was accepted in that state. How does one "accept" an offer? By communicating her acceptance of the offer, or of her intention to now buy or sell the securities pursuant to said offer.

Oops, sorry. A little legalese just leaked out that time.

So, if an offer to sell comes from State A and is directed to a client in State B, an offer to sell has now been "made" in both states. And the Administrators of both states have jurisdiction over any funny stuff.

If it's an offer to *buy*, however, the offer would have to be accepted before that state's securities Administrator has authority. Not surprisingly, the regulators get more nervous when somebody tries to sell something (offer to sell) than when somebody tries to buy (offer to buy) something.

An offer has been directed into/received in a state if mail is sent to a post office in the state. So if a registered rep sends the offer by mail, and the offer is delivered to a post office box in Kentucky, the offer has now been directed into/received in the state of Kentucky, even if the owner of the PO box is on vacation in another state at the time or has since moved to Tennessee.

So that's when an offer has been made in a state, which, of course, means we now have to establish when an offer has NOT been made in a state.

Bet you can't wait, huh? Oh well. Here goes.

The USA clearly states that an offer to sell or to buy is NOT considered to be made in "this state" if:

(1)   the publisher circulates in this state any bona fide newspaper or other publication of general, regular, and paid circulation which is not published in the state or which *is* published in this state but has had more than two-thirds (66.7%) of its circulation outside this state during the past twelve months

(2)   a radio or television program originating outside this state is received in this state

So when a resident of Illinois picks up a newspaper or periodical published in the state of Wisconsin and sees an offer to sell securities, that offer is not considered to have been made in Illinois.

Where the heck WAS it made then?

Wisconsin. So the Wisconsin Administrator has jurisdiction over that offer. But, if the alert newspaper reader then calls the number in the advertisement and says he/she would like to buy some of them-there securities, and the seller—presumably—accepts the opportunity to sell some of them-there securities, now an offer to buy has been made and accepted in the state of Illinois, so the powers of the IL Administrator kick in. So, when the advertisement was sent into Illinois via the out-of-state newspaper, no offer to sell had been made in Illinois. However, if somebody in IL reads the offer, calls the number in the ad and says they'd like to buy the securities—and the seller accepts, as sellers are prone to do—now an offer to buy has been made and accepted in the state of Illinois.

The next clause means that if the periodical is published in the state of Illinois but 2/3 or more of the circulation is OUTSIDE the state of Illinois, then any offer published is NOT considered to have originated in Illinois.

And, if a radio or TV ad is broadcast into Illinois, the offer is not considered to have been made in the state of Illinois. Rather, it is an offer in the state where the microphone/TV cameras are located.

Aren't you glad you know that? Won't that make you a much more successful registered representative?

Civil liabilities. A registered rep or broker-dealer can also be subject to civil liabilities. If a broker-dealer sells a customer an unregistered, non-exempt security, the customer could sue to recover damages, including reasonable attorney fees and court costs. The seller of that security is liable for the price the customer paid, plus interest, but minus any dividend or interest payment the customer might have received from the security in the meantime. In other words, if the unregistered, non-exempt security were sold for $10, the firm would have to repurchase the stock at $10, plus interest. If the stock had paid $1 in dividends, the firm would deduct $1 from what they pay the customer. Same thing if it turned out the agent sold a security when *he* wasn't registered.

The statute of limitations for money disputes/civil matters is a little tricky. It's basically two years from the date of the unlawful sale, so if the customer knew about it for 25 months, it's too late to sue. If the seller concealed the illegality from the customer, or the customer could not reasonably be expected to know something funky was afoot, there would be another year tacked on, but after three years it's too late to sue.

So, for criminal violations, the statue is five years. For civil liability, the statute is two years from discovery, or three years from the event, whichever comes first.

If the registered rep realizes her mistake of selling a client a non-exempt security that should have been registered, she can make what's known as an offer of **rescission**. Sort of like a "do-over" that satisfies the requirements of the USA. Here, the rep offers to repurchase the stock for the price paid, plus interest, minus any dividends or interest income that may have been received. If the customer receives the written offer and 30 days have gone by, it's too late to sue. So the customer either accepts the offer, or decides to sue. She has 30 days to do something.

Exempt Transactions

The following <u>transactions</u> are exempt and, therefore, the securities sold in these transactions do not have to be registered with the state Administrator:

- isolated nonissuer transactions in outstanding securities
- nonissuer transactions in securities traded publicly at least 90 days
- nonissuer transactions in securities subject to reporting requirements of the Exchange Act of 1934 that have publicly traded 180 days
- unsolicited nonissuer orders
- underwriter transactions
- transactions by fiduciaries: executors, Administrators, sheriffs, marshals, receivers/trustees
- pledges
- transactions with financial institutions
- private placements

No more than 10 non-institutional buyers in the state per 12-month period

- offerings of pre-organization certificates to no more than 10 persons
- offerings to existing shareholders

If a security is sold in any of these exempt transactions, it doesn't matter if it's registered or not.

Let's say you're the registered representative. Somebody calls you up and wants to buy 1,000 shares of a small manufacturing company headquartered in Terre Haute, Indiana. As an agent in San Antonio, Texas, you don't know too much about this manufacturing company in Indiana, but the numbers look right, and you aren't in the habit of refusing orders in the first place. So, you sell the stock to your customer and pocket a decent commission. Three months later, you discover that stock was only registered in Indiana, because it was originally sold in an "intrastate" offering, going only to Indiana residents.

Oops. That stock was never registered in Texas, where your client lives and you do business.

Oh well. The sale wasn't your idea to begin with. It was all your customer's notion. Your customer called you, so it's an "unsolicited transaction."

Bingo—that makes it an exempt transaction, so it doesn't matter that the stock wasn't registered.

Now, if this had been your idea—ouch! That's a prohibited practice that could get your license suspended or revoked by the Administrator in Texas.

But unsolicited transactions are exempt, meaning if the stock isn't registered, oh well.

See, the Administrators are more nervous about agents trying to SELL, than they are about customers trying to BUY. As Elvis' bodyguard said, "How do you protect a man from himself?"

You can't. You have to let people do pretty much what they want to do, as long as it ain't hurtin' nobody.

But, if somebody is trying to SELL something to a resident of the state, that's when the state gets all nervous and regulatory, because sales reps can and do hurt people all the time. The distinction between solicited and un-solicited is so important the Administrator might require a formal document with the customer's signature indicating that this was, in fact, the customer's idea, not the representative's.

Other transactions are exempt, so if the security turns out to be unregistered, oh well. Doesn't have to be registered, since the transaction qualifies for an exemption. If an issuer sells to an underwriter, the security doesn't have to be registered yet. It has to be registered before the public buys it, not before the underwriters take possession of it. Any transaction between an issuer and a financial institution or an institutional buyer is an exempt transaction, since these are sophisticated, professional investors. If a fiduciary is selling off assets (sheriff, marshal, trustee, executor), the security doesn't have to be registered. Those folks aren't securities dealers, and they're going by the book in a very public fashion, anyway. Just liquidating assets because somebody got arrested, went bankrupt, or went to meet that final margin call in the sky.

And since the Administrator is such a regular guy, he's even going to let each broker-dealer do one or two transactions per year in the secondary market even when the stock isn't registered in the state. Those are called isolated, non-issuer transactions. No one is raising capital for a business—just selling stock between two investors. As long as it doesn't happen more than once or twice a year per firm, we're okay with it.

So, yes, there are plenty of times when a stock doesn't have to be registered, but if it *does* have to be registered—because it just can't find an exemption—then woe unto he or she who tries to sell it in the state! Of course, if you can't find an exemption from registration, chances are, you just aren't trying hard enough, but that's a different matter.

Also remember that the Administrator—if he has a real good reason—can revoke any of the exemptions granted those exciting transactions we just looked at. And, he can even revoke the exemption from state filing requirements for two specific types of otherwise exempt securities: non-profit securities and securities issued in connection with an employee benefit plan.

Basically, just remember that on the exam, all securities have to be registered in all cases, except in all the cases when they don't.

Are we having fun yet?

Answers to All Review Questions

1. ANSWER: D

EXPLANATION: as soon as you see "a broker-dealer," you can eliminate choices A and B, since broker-dealers are NEVER agents and vice versa. C is also eliminated as soon as you see that the individual represents an exempt issuer, Uncle Sam. As soon as you see that the individual represents a broker-dealer, you know he/she is an agent, regardless of what he/she sells.

2. ANSWER: D

EXPLANATION: none of these folks is an agent. Again, broker-dealers are NOT agents, so A and B are eliminated. Choice C is also not an agent because the individual has <u>no office in the state</u> and deals with a client who is not a resident (< 30 days). Note that if the individual *had* an office in the state, he/she *would* be an agent, end of story.

3. ANSWER: C

EXPLANATION: only the bonds issued by the *national* government of Mexico would be exempt, so if the individual sells bonds issued by a local or provincial government of Mexico, he/she IS an agent. Note that ALL governments (not corporations) of Canada are exempt issuers. Canada is special. Mexico is not. The law does not have to be logical. It is what it is.

4. ANSWER: D

EXPLANATION: A is a prohibited practice known as "commingling." B violates the suitability requirements for two reasons: 1) low tax bracket investors should NOT buy municipal bonds, since they don't have a tax problem to begin with and 2) bonds do not provide growth; they provide income. C is bad because munibonds don't go in retirement accounts—otherwise the individual would end up paying tax on the income at distribution. D is tricky. The individual did NOT ignore a client's instructions, which is good. Had he ignored the instructions, he would have committed a prohibited practice.

5. ANSWER: D

EXPLANATION: T-bonds are perfectly suitable for a risk-averse investor, but the agent goofed when he said they carry no risk. Although the client will not lose her principal, she could still end up buying a bond at, say, $980 and then watch interest rates climb, pushing the price down to, say, $700. If she wanted to sell the bond, she'd be SOL.

6. ANSWER: C

EXPLANATION: don't trust the words used on the exam. "Omitting an immaterial fact" might sound bad . . . until you break down the word im-material. You should omit im-material facts, because they have nothing to do with the investment. Omitting a material—important, relevant—fact is fraudulent. Customers claim all kinds of things—that don't make it fraud.

7. ANSWER: B

EXPLANATION: as long as both agents are registered, it's okay to share commissions. The Administrator—just like the SEC—neither approves nor disapproves. They both either allow or disallow. No approval being granted from those regulators. Never ignore a customer's explicit instructions, and don't promise to perform tasks you're not likely or able to perform.

8. ANSWER: B

EXPLANATION: gotta break down the words. An "exempt" security doesn't have to be registered, so it's okay to solicit orders for it. If it's "non-exempt" it has to be registered. For C/D, does it really matter what the agent "intends" to do after he/she has illegally commingled assets?

Nope.

9. ANSWER: C

EXPLANATION: you have to state the material/relevant facts . . . not ALL facts about a security. The other stuff don't even sound right, does it?

10. ANSWER: B

EXPLANATION: choice "A" represents a prohibited practice, but if it wasn't intentional, it wasn't fraud. Choice "C" should remind you that only the material facts need to be communicated to the prospect/client. And choice "B" should jump off the page at you—lying about the amount you're charging a customer?

Wow, dude, that's, like, big-time fraud!

11. ANSWER: C

EXPLANATION: it isn't ethical to lie about your credentials. It's okay to charge higher commissions and markups than usual, as long as the client has given his/her consent.

12. ANSWER: D

EXPLANATION: current yield is only dividends divided by POP. Never combine capital gains distributions with it, and always clearly explain the terminology to customers. If you're going to compare something to a CD or insured bank product, you have to also point out that this thing you're comparing doesn't come with the FDIC insurance/guarantee that bank products offer. And choice "C" pretty much speaks for itself.

13. ANSWER: D

EXPLANATION: that statute of limitations is 5 years (choice B is trying to confuse criminal with civil statutes of limitations), and ignorance of the law, if proven by the ignorant party publicly proving his/her ignorance, can keep the ignorant party out of jail. They might still pay a fine, but no jail time.

14. ANSWER: C

EXPLANATION: just eliminate A, B, and D. Issuers, banks, and agents are NOT broker-dealers, end of story. C is the textbook definition of a B/D.

15. ANSWER: C

EXPLANATION: if they have an office in the state, they register. If they don't have an office in the state, they might not have to register. **A** does not have to register because they aren't in the state of Kentucky and are only dealing with pension funds—the number of pension funds is irrelevant. B does not have to register because they aren't located in Arizona and are only dealing with banks and S&L's—again the number is irrelevant. D also does not have to register because they aren't located in the state and are selling to an existing client not a resident of the state.

16. ANSWER: D

EXPLANATION: an "agent" is NOT a broker-dealer, and neither is a bank. They are defined, rather, as "agents" and "banks," respectively.

If the firm has no office in the state, they aren't broker-dealers if they deal with institutional investors. They can deal with 5 non-accredited/institutional investors, but if the number is "7," then they ARE defined as a broker-dealer in the state.

17. ANSWER: B

EXPLANATION: not ALL lawyers are exempt. If the lawyer does actually provide advice for a separate fee, he/she is an investment adviser. Investment adviser representatives are NOT investment advisers and vice versa (just like agents are not B/D's and vice versa). The investment adviser is almost always a firm—the rep is the individual who works for the firm. A federal covered adviser can not be defined as an investment adviser at the state/Uniform Securities Act level.

18. ANSWER: C

EXPLANATION: memorize this information and keep moving

19. ANSWER: D

EXPLANATION: federal covered advisers have to do choices A-C, but they aren't under the regular watchful eye of the Administrator, so they don't have to submit to surprise inspections. The Administrator just wants to know they're in the state, and will only go after them in the event of fraud. Cause they'll go after just about anybody in the even of fraud.

20. ANSWER: B

EXPLANATION: if the lawyer is charging a fee for specific advice, that makes him/her an adviser. They'd have to register. "Reps" are never advisers, so eliminate choice A. A "federal covered" adviser is defined as an adviser at the federal level, not the state/USA level.

21. ANSWER: D

EXPLANATION: investment adviser reps always register in the state in which they do business—only the firm can be federal covered, not the rep. As soon as the firm sends communications to more than 5 non-institutional clients in a state, the firm has to register in that state. The adviser in Mississippi is doing business in Mississippi, right? End of story.

22. ANSWER: C

EXPLANATION: if there's no rule against it, the adviser can take custody as long as the Administrator is informed. See, the Administrator might wanna have a look-see some afternoon, just to make sure the money/securities are actually in custody and no funny business is going on.

23. ANSWER: A

EXPLANATION: since the information is IM-material, it doesn't matter. If the agent omitted or made an untrue statement of <u>material</u> fact, he/she would be in trouble, of course. B, C, D are all prohibited.

24. ANSWER: D

EXPLANATION: A is false because D is true. B is false because the statements must be sent quarterly. C is false because the inspection can't be arranged—it has to be a surprise inspection.

25. ANSWER: C

EXPLANATION: choice C is a textbook description of what an advisory contract has to be. A is prohibited because the advisor has to be compensated by a percentage of assets over a specified time frame, not compensated just because of one big gain on one stock. Contracts must be in writing, and you don't disclose your clients' affairs unless your clients give consent or a court order forces you to disclose them.

26. ANSWER: C

EXPLANATION: 3 years, $5,000. Memorize it and move on.

27. ANSWER: C

EXPLANATION: only a pending registration can be summarily suspended without prior notice and opportunity for hearing. A cease and desist order can be issued without prior notice and opportunity for hearing, but a stop order can not. The Administrator can NOT issue an injunction—only a court can do that.

28. ANSWER: D

EXPLANATION: the Administrator can do all of the activities mentioned except sentence violators to prison. He'd have to get a court to do that.

29. ANSWER: C

EXPLANATION: whiskey warehouse receipts and interests in multilevel distributorships are securities, but fixed annuities are not. To answer these questions, just remember what a security is NOT. It does not have a fixed payment, is not a commodity/precious metal. So, if it's not a fixed payment or a commodity, it IS a security.

30. ANSWER: C

EXPLANATION: variable annuities are securities (fixed annuities are not). In "A" we might be talking about a security, but B/D's are not agents. Donating is not the same thing as selling, which is why choice B is not in the answer.

31. ANSWER: D

EXPLANATION: fraud is the willful/intentional attempt to deceive. Selling unregistered securities that have no exemption (non-exempt) is prohibited, but since the agent didn't mean to do it, it's not fraudulent. It is prohibited but not fraudulent under USA; the fact that the client is a high net worth individual is irrelevant.

32. ANSWER: D

EXPLANATION: none of these activities is prohibited. Im-material facts should be omitted, since they aren't material or important to the investment decision. There is no set number of transactions that may be undertaken, especially for clients with a high risk tolerance. In choice C the security did not have to be registered, since it has an exemption from registration.

33. ANSWER: D

EXPLANATION: those are all sales and all securities, right?

34. ANSWER: D

EXPLANATION: none of these statements is true. Nothing is effective a certain number of days *after* anything. It's either effective concurrently with federal (coordination, filing) or whenever the Administrator so orders (qualification). IPO's are usually done by coordinating the federal registration with state registration.

35. ANSWER: A

EXPLANATION: the Administrator wants to know WHERE you will be selling and how much you will sell in HIS state. Not how much you will sell in *other* states.

36. ANSWER: D

EXPLANATION: if the issuer hasn't filed a registration statement with the SEC, it will have to register by qualification. If the corporation has only been in business 2

½ years (we need 36 consecutive months), they can not register by filing and, therefore, must register by qualification. In choice C the issuer will register with the Administrator, since they're only selling in one state.

NASAA STATEMENTS OF POLICY AND MODEL RULES

At www.nasaa.org under "nasaa library" you will find adopted statements of policy and adopted model rules. NASAA says that these are also "fair game" on the exam, as well as anything covered by the Uniform Securities Act.

No one can tell you, "This WILL be on the test and this WON'T be on the test." So, you should probably read ALL the statements of policy and model rules.

What I've done here is include the most likely statements of policy to appear on the exam. By far, I think the most "testable" statement is called "Dishonest or Unethical Business Practices of Broker-Dealers and Agents," adopted in 1983. Since the exam is most concerned with business practices, you can safely assume that several questions will come from this statement of policy.

So, we'll start with that one and also dissect three more.

That doesn't mean you shouldn't read the others—we have to make an educated guess as to what will show up on the exam, and that's what we've done. If we covered every factoid that "could" show up on the test, we'd be studying for three years, no exaggeration.

And nobody wants that.

So, make sure you know the USA inside out. Make sure you can spot the no-no's a mile away. Understand what the Administrator can do to make your life difficult. And read the most "testable" policy statements.

Then go in and kick that little exam's you-know-what.

DISHONEST OR UNETHICAL BUSINESS PRACTICES OF BROKER-DEALERS AND AGENTS

[Adopted May 23, 1983]

[HIGH STANDARDS AND JUST PRINCIPLES.] Each broker-dealer and agent shall observe high standards of commercial honor and just and equitable principles of trade in the conduct of their business. Acts and practices, including but not limited to the following, are considered contrary to such standards and may constitute grounds for denial, suspension or revocation of registration or such other action authorized by statute.

1. BROKER-DEALERS

a. Engaging in a pattern of unreasonable and unjustifiable delays in the delivery of securities purchased by any of its customers and/or in the payment upon request of free credit balances reflecting completed transactions of any of its customers;

b. Inducing trading in a customer's account which is excessive in size or frequency in view of the financial resources and character of the account;

c. Recommending to a customer the purchase, sale or exchange of any security without reasonable grounds to believe that such transaction or recommendation is suitable for the customer based upon reasonable inquiry concerning the customer's investment objectives, financial situation and needs, and any other relevant information known by the broker-dealer;

d. Executing a transaction on behalf of a customer without authorization to do so;

e. Exercising any discretionary power in effecting a transaction for a customer's account without first obtaining written discretionary authority from the customer, unless the discretionary power relates solely to the time and/or price for the executing of orders;

f. Executing any transaction in a margin account without securing from the customer a properly executed written margin agreement promptly after the initial transaction in the account;

g. Failing to segregate customers' free securities or securities held in safekeeping;

h. Hypothecating a customer's securities without having a lien thereon unless the broker-dealer secures from the customer a properly executed written consent promptly after the initial transaction, except as permitted by Rules of the Securities and Exchange Commission;

i. Entering into a transaction with or for a customer at a price not reasonably related to the current market price of the security or receiving an unreasonable commission or profit;

j. Failing to furnish to a customer purchasing securities in an offering, no later than the due date of confirmation of the transaction, either a final prospectus or a preliminary prospectus and an additional document, which together include all information set forth in the final prospectus;

k. Charging unreasonable and inequitable fees for services performed, including miscellaneous services such as collection of monies due for principal, dividends or interest, exchange or transfer of securities, appraisals, safekeeping, or custody of securities and other services related to its securities business;

l. Offering to buy from or sell to any person any security at a stated price unless such brokerdealer is prepared to purchase or sell, as the case may be, at such price and under such conditions as are stated at the time of such offer to buy or sell;

m. Representing that a security is being offered to a customer "at the market" or a price relevant to the market price unless such broker-dealer knows or has reasonable grounds to believe that a market for such security exists other than that made, created or controlled by such brokerdealer, or by any such person for whom he is acting or with whom he is associated in such distribution, or any person controlled by, controlling or under common control with such broker-dealer;

n. Effecting any transaction in, or inducing the purchase or sale of, any security by means of any manipulative, deceptive or fraudulent device, practice, plan, program, design or contrivance, which may include but not be limited to;

(1) Effecting any transaction in a security which involves no change in the beneficial ownership thereof;

(2) Entering an order or orders for the purchase or sale of any security with the knowledge that an order or orders of substantially the same size, at substantially the same time and substantially the same price, for the sale of any such security, has been or will be entered by or for the same or different parties for the purpose of creating a false or misleading appearance of active trading in the security or a false or misleading

appearance with respect to the market for the security; provided, however, nothing in this subsection shall prohibit a broker-dealer from entering bona fide agency cross transactions for its customers;

(3) Effecting, alone or with one or more other persons, a series of transactions in any security creating actual or apparent active trading in such security or raising or depressing the price of such security, for the purpose of inducing the purchase or sale of such security by others;

o. Guaranteeing a customer against loss in any securities account of such customer carried by the broker-dealer or in any securities transaction effected by the broker-dealer or in any securities transaction effected by the broker-dealer with or for such customer;

p. Publishing or circulating, or causing to be published or circulated, any notice, circular, advertisement, newspaper article, investment service, or communication of any kind which purports to report any transaction as a purchase or sale of any security unless such brokerdealer believes that such transaction was a bona fide purchase or sale or such security; or which purports to quote the bid price or asked price for any security, unless such brokerdealer believes that such quotation represents a bona fide bid for, or offer of, such security;

q. Using any advertising or sales presentation in such a fashion as to be deceptive or misleading. An example of such practice would be a distribution of any nonfactual data, material or presentation based on conjecture, unfounded or unrealistic claims or assertions in any brochure, flyer, or display by words, pictures, graphs or otherwise designed to supplement, detract from, supersede or defeat the purpose or effect of any prospectus or disclosure; or

r. Failing to disclose that the broker-dealer is controlled by, controlling, affiliated with or under common control with the issuer of any security before entering into any contract with or for a customer for the purchase or sale of such security, the existence of such control to such customer, and if such disclosure is not made in writing, it shall be supplemented by the giving or sending of written disclosure at or before the completion of the transaction;

s. Failing to make a bona fide public offering of all of the securities allotted to a broker-dealer for distribution, whether acquired as an underwriter, a selling group member, or from a member participating in the distribution as an underwriter or selling group member; or

t. Failure or refusal to furnish a customer, upon reasonable request, information to which he is entitled, or to respond to a formal written request or complaint.

2. AGENTS

a. Engaging in the practice of lending or borrowing money or securities from a customer, or acting as a custodian for money, securities or an executed stock power of a customer;

b. Effecting securities transactions not recorded on the regular books or records of the brokerdealer which the agent represents, unless the transactions are authorized in writing by the broker-dealer prior to execution of the transaction;

c. Establishing or maintaining an account containing fictitious information in order to execute transactions which would otherwise be prohibited;

d. Sharing directly or indirectly in profits or losses in the account of any customer without the written authorization of the customer and the broker-dealer which the agent represents;

e. Dividing or otherwise splitting the agent's commissions, profits or other compensation from the purchase or sale of securities with any person not also registered as an agent for the same broker-dealer, or for a broker-dealer under direct or indirect common control; or

f. Engaging in conduct specified in Subsection 1.b, c, d, e, f, i, j, n, o, p, or q.

[CONDUCT NOT INCLUSIVE.] The conduct set forth above is not inclusive. Engaging in other conduct such as forgery, embezzlement, nondisclosure, incomplete disclosure or misstatement of material facts, or manipulative or deceptive practices shall also be grounds for denial, suspension or revocation of registration.

ONCE AGAIN, IN ENGLISH, PLEASE...

The following explanation should help to de-code some of the previous legalese.

NASAA Adopted Statement of Policy   5/23/1983
Dishonest or Unethical Business Practices of Broker-Dealers and Agents

This policy statement looks like extremely fertile ground for harvesting test questions. Business practices make up the biggest section on the exam, and this policy statement lists a whole bunch of prohibited practices that can lead to a registration for a broker-dealer or agent being denied, suspended, or revoked.

Which is bad.

The policy statement starts with the conduct of **broker-dealers**.

Item A says, "Don't be dragging your feet when your customer buys or sells securities." Send them their securities or their money within a reasonable time frame. What's reasonable? Would you like to hold a hearing to determine what's reasonable?

Probably a much better idea to be prompt forking over your customers' cash and securities.

Item B demonstrates how 24 big words can be easily boiled down into just one word: churning.

Don't do that.

And if you do do that, make sure you don't get caught. As of January 11, 2002 churning is punishable by 7 years in federal prison or death by firing squad.

Seriously.

Also, notice how churning is not just excessive *frequency*, but excessive size, too. So, don't pressure customers into making bigger trades just because it leads to bigger commissions or markups for the firm. Item C is just a reminder to perform due diligence when determining suitability. Your recommendations don't have to be profitable—no one can predict the future—but they do have to make sense given each customer's situation. Item D reminds the firm not to buy or sell securities for a customer if the customer hasn't authorized the broker-dealer to do so. You'd think that would not even have to be articulated, but it's actually a surprisingly common occurrence by unscrupulous firms. Nobody's calling to trade? Let's trade *for* them.

No. You have to have discretion over the account to trade without talking to the customer first, and even then you have to buy what's suitable for the client given her investment objectives, risk tolerance, time horizon, etc. Item E is very closely related. Where Item D focuses on the transaction, Item E says "any discretionary power," which could be broken down into the three basic aspects that make an order "discretionary." As you recall from the 6, 7 or 65, choosing the activity (buy/sell), asset (which stock/bond), or the amount (# of shares/bonds) makes an order discretionary. So, if the firm does not have <u>written</u> discretionary authorization from the customer before making any of those choices, they've made a big boo-boo. They can choose time and/or price, because those aspects are not considered discretionary. And—unfortunately—this concept can be tricky. Remember, this statement is talking to <u>broker-dealers</u>, not investment advisers. An IA can actually start using discretion once they've received verbal authorization, provided they get the discretionary authorization in writing within 10 business days. So, be real clear on whether the question is talking to a firm called a broker-dealer or a firm called an investment adviser. I guess an IA, being a "fiduciary," is already expected to act completely for his customer's best interest, so the rule is a little more lax there?

Not that it matters. It's the rule because the regulators say so. And it'll remain the rule until, by rule, they change their mind.

Item F reminds the firm not to let a customer start trading on margin unless they have a signed margin agreement promptly after the initial transaction. I would have expected the rule to require the agreement ahead of time, but nobody asked my opinion. This is an example, though, of where your gut feeling could be wrong. You expect the regulators to be uptight about everything, but that's not always the case. The signed margin agreement has to come promptly *after* the first transaction on margin.

Hmm. Oh well. It is what it is.

Point G reminds the firm exactly what the Act of 1934 tried to remind them—commingling is a no-no. Keep the customers' securities separate from the firms' securities. Point H tells the firm to go by the books when pledging customer securities as collateral, which is what you do in a margin account. Point I takes all the fun out of the business by prohibiting the time-honored tradition of sticking it to the customer, gouging him at every opportunity. Point J could also be a test question on the Series 7 or 6—the final prospectus for new offerings must be delivered no later than confirmation of the sale. The customer has already received a preliminary prospectus (Red Herring) but must get the final (or the preliminary plus any additional info) no later than confirmation. See, often the preliminary is so close to the final that they just give an additional statement to it and that serves as the final prospectus.

No, nothing is simple in this business. Except for the simple stuff.

Item K sounds just like the bylaws of the NASD—you can't charge unreasonable fees for services rendered. What makes it unreasonable?

Would you like to hold a hearing?

Point L goes way overboard. Point L has the audacity to dictate to a broker-dealer that they can't tell a customer they'll purchase 1,000 shares of XYZ for $45 a share then try to hand them $22 a share when the deal actually goes down five minutes later.

It's getting to where I don't know how anyone is expected to make a living in this business!

Anyway, item M is little dense. Basically, it's saying that the firm probably shouldn't tell the customer that the firm is purchasing the customer's security "at the market" unless the firm has reasonable grounds to believe that there is, like, an actual "market" for the security outside whatever price the firm decides is fair.

Kind of surprising that some of these rules have to be written, but we don't live in a perfect world.

Item N goes into great detail in explaining that market manipulation will get you into all kinds of trouble. We can't just get together with another firm and start creating the illusion of an active market for a particular stock, no matter how much fun it would be. Words like pegging, capping, painting the tape, matched purchases, and wash sales all fall under this category of market manipulation. Unless you want to lose your license and work in the prison library, I'd recommend staying away from any of that stuff.

Item O reminds the firm not to guarantee the customer against loss. Now there's a rule I can live with, right? Since no one can do it, I don't have to worry about my competitors offering guarantees, either.

Item P is just a dense, legalistic way of saying don't publish in any way, shape, or form that a transaction has occurred unless you actually know it occurred.

Hmm, seems reasonable enough to me.

Item Q reminds the firm not to circulate material that is misleading or deceptive. For example, it might be tempting to put out a flyer that shows how much Company XYZ would be worth if over the next 6 months they simply eliminated $5 billion in debt, increased revenues 10,000% and slashed costs 89% without resorting to layoffs or pay-cuts. You could even show graphs of this wonderful turnaround effort. Trouble is, it's all based on wild conjecture, is so improbable as to be nearly impossible and, therefore, should not be circulated at all. It is "nonfactual," misleading and probably deceptive.

Don't do that.

Item R is pretty clear as-is. If the firm wants to sell shares of an issuer who just happens to own, control, or be affiliated with the broker-dealer, that should maybe be disclosed to the customer and explained clearly. We aren't just making a commission, markup or spread on this sale—we're actually directly related to the issuer getting the proceeds. That just might explain our intense enthusiasm of this particular offering.

Item S reminds underwriters not to get greedy when they see the price of an IPO stock start to soar in the secondary market. Might be tempting to withhold the securities just to see how high the price could soar, but that would be "failure to make a bona fide offering" and would get the firm into all kinds of trouble.

Item T is about as clear as NASAA's legalese will ever get. A principal of the broker-dealer has to respond to a customer's written complaint, and has to provide him with any information to which he is entitled. Like a balance sheet, for example. You feel embarrassed by the liabilities on the firm's balance sheet—too bad, the rule says you have to provide the balance sheet to the customer upon the request.

AGENTS.

And then the policy statement proceeds to tell agents what's what.

Not sure why you'd want to, but don't act as a custodian for your client. Don't, like, take their cash or stock certificates and, like, put them in your glove box or top desk drawer. Don't borrow or lend money/securities with/to your client. You make recommendations; they buy and sell.

Keep it simple and everybody's happy. Don't start acting like a bank. You're not a bank; you're an agent.

Remember that.

My father was a small businessman who didn't know much about accounting, but he always told me to keep two sets of books as I recall.

Not.

Don't effect (complete) transactions not recorded on the books of your firm unless you have written authorization from the firm to do so. That also sounds bizarre—that it's okay if your firm puts it in writing. This would be about the *only* place on the exam where I'd say that getting the firm's permission in writing makes it okay.

Item C is self-explanatory. Fictitious accounts?

Wow.

Item D reminds us that, basically, you shouldn't be sharing profits and/or losses with a customer. The only exception is when you're in a joint account with the customer and you've received the customer's authorization as well as your broker-dealer's. Gotta have both the customer's and the B/D's written authorization. If you get any test question on the sharing arrangement, remember that you must share in proportion to your investment in the account.

Item E makes it clear that you can only split commissions with registered agents at your firm or a firm directly related to your firm, as a subsidiary, for example. So, you can split commissions, as long as the agent is registered and works for your firm directly or indirectly.

The policy statement then tells the agent not to do the stuff it told broker-dealers not to do, except for the stuff that would only relate to the firm.

And then the policy statement ends with a reminder that these prohibited activities are not inclusive, meaning there's still lots of other stuff that could get you in hot water with the regulators. They just felt like pointing out SOME of the things not to do in this policy statement.

UNETHICAL BUSINESS PRACTICES OF INVESTMENT ADVISERS

Amended 4/27/1997, Adopted in 1985

A person who is an investment adviser or a federal covered adviser is a fiduciary and has a duty to act primarily for the benefit of its clients. The provisions of this subsection apply to federal covered advisers to the extent that the conduct alleged is fraudulent, deceptive, or as otherwise permitted by the National Securities Markets Improvement Act of 1996 Pub. L. No. 104-290). While the extent and nature of this duty varies according to the nature of the relationship between an investment adviser and its clients and the circumstances of each case, an investment adviser or a federal covered adviser shall not engage in unethical business practices, including the following:

1.   Recommending to a client to whom supervisory, management or consulting services are provided the purchase, sale or exchange of any security without reasonable grounds to believe that the recommendation is suitable for the client on the basis of information furnished by the client after reasonable inquiry concerning the client's investment objectives, financial situation and needs, and any other information known by the investment adviser.

2.   Exercising any discretionary power in placing an order for the purchase or sale of securities for a client without obtaining written discretionary authority from the client within ten (10) business days after the date of the first transaction placed pursuant to oral discretionary authority, unless the discretionary power relates solely to the price at which, or the time when, an order involving a definite amount of a specified security shall be executed, or both.

3.   Inducing trading in a client's account that is excessive in size or frequency in view of the financial resources, investment objectives and character of the account in light of the fact that an adviser in such situations can directly benefit from the number of securities transactions effected in a client's account. The rule appropriately forbids an excessive number of transaction orders to be induced by an adviser for a "customer's account."

4.   Placing an order to purchase or sell a security for the account of a client without authority to do so.

5. Placing an order to purchase or sell a security for the account of a client upon instruction of a third party without first having obtained a written third-party trading authorization from the client. Borrowing money or securities from a client unless the client is a broker-dealer, an affiliate of the investment adviser, or a financial institution engaged in the business of loaning funds.

7. Loaning money to a client unless the investment adviser is a financial institution engaged in the business of loaning funds or the client is an affiliate of the investment adviser.

8. To misrepresent to any advisory client, or prospective advisory client, the qualifications of the investment adviser or any employee of the investment adviser, or to misrepresent the nature of the advisory services being offered or fees to be charged for such service, or to omit to state a material fact necessary to make the statements made regarding qualifications, services or fees, in light of the circumstances under which they are made, not misleading.

9. Providing a report or recommendation to any advisory client prepared by someone other than the adviser without disclosing that fact. (This prohibition does not apply to a situation where the adviser uses published research reports or statistical analyses to render advice or where an adviser orders such a report in the normal course of providing service.)

10. Charging a client an unreasonable advisory fee.

11. Failing to disclose to clients in writing before any advice is rendered any material conflict of interest relating to the adviser or any of its employees which could reasonably be expected to impair the rendering of unbiased and objective advice including:

(a) Compensation arrangements connected with advisory services to clients which are in addition to compensation from such clients for such services; and

(b) Charging a client an advisory fee for rendering advice when a commission for executing securities transactions pursuant to such advice will be received by the

12. Guaranteeing a client that a specific result will be achieved (gain or no loss) with advice which will be rendered.

13. Publishing, circulating or distributing any advertisement which does not comply with Rule 206 (4)-1 under the Investment Advisers Act of 1940.

14. Disclose the identity, affairs, or investments of any client unless required by law to do so, or unless consented to by the client.

15. Taking any action, directly or indirectly, with respect to those securities or funds in which any client has any beneficial interest, where the investment adviser has custody or possession of such securities or funds when the advisor's action is subject to and does not comply with the requirements of Reg. 206 (4)-2 under the Investment Advisers Act of 1940.

16. Entering into, extending or renewing any investment advisory contract unless such contract is in writing and discloses, in substance, the services to be provided, the term of the contract, the advisory fee, the formula for computing the fee, the amount of prepaid fee to be returned in the event of contract termination or nonperformance, whether the contract grants discretionary power to the adviser and that no assignment of such contract shall be made by the investment adviser without the consent of the other party to the contract.

17. Failing to establish, maintain, and enforce written policies and procedures reasonably designed to prevent the misuse of material nonpublic information contrary to the provisions of Section 204A of the Investment Advisers Act of 1940.

18. Entering into, extending, or renewing any advisory contract contrary to the provisions of section 205 of the Investment Advisers Act of 1940. This provision shall apply to all advisers registered or required to be registered under this Act, notwithstanding whether such adviser would be exempt from federal registration pursuant to section 203 (b) of the Investment Advisers Act of 1940.

19. To indicate, in an advisory contract, any condition, stipulation, or provisions binding any person to waive compliance with any provision of this act or of the Investment Advisers Act of 1940, or any other practice contrary to the provisions of section 215 of the Investment Advisers Act of 1940.

20. Engaging in any act, practice, or course of business which is fraudulent, deceptive, or manipulative in contrary to the provisions of section 206 (4) of the Investment Advisers Act of 1940, notwithstanding the fact that such investment adviser is not registered or required to be registered under section 203 of the Investment Advisers Act of 1940.

21. Engaging in conduct or any act, indirectly or through or by any other person, which would be unlawful for such person to do directly under the provisions of this act or any rule or regulation there under. The conduct set forth above is not inclusive. Engaging in other conduct such as nondisclosure, incomplete disclosure, or deceptive practices shall be deemed an unethical business practice. The federal statutory and

regulatory provisions referenced herein shall apply to investment advisers and federal covered advisers, to the extent permitted by the National Securities Markets Improvement Act of 1996 (Pub. L. No. l04-290).

Plain English Version

NASAA Adopted Model Rule:
Unethical Business Practices of Investment Advisers
Amended 4/27/1997, Adopted in 1985

The first point this adopted model rule makes is that <u>an investment adviser is a fiduciary and has a duty to act primarily for the benefit of its clients</u>. Of course, that's basically the definition of the word *fiduciary*: someone who has a duty to act primarily for the benefit of someone else. Remember that a custodian is a fiduciary for the minor in an UGMA account. Same way a trustee is a fiduciary for the beneficial owner of the trust account, or a pension fund manager is a fiduciary for all the pensioners in the plan. If we break down the word <u>fi</u>duciary, we see the same root used in the word "<u>fi</u>delity," or "in<u>fi</u>delity," which represent the difference between marital bliss and a quick trip to divorce court. A husband must be <u>faithful</u> to his wife, as a trustee must be <u>faithful</u> to the beneficial owner of the trust account. Fiduciaries must be faithful, show *fidelity*.

At the risk of digressing, other words that have "fid" in them all have something to do with faithful or true:

- Fido (name of a pet dog)
- Semper Fidelis (always true, US Marine Corps)
- Bona Fide (good, authentic, true, as in "bona fide contract")

Why are they telling you that an adviser is a fiduciary? First, it reminds advisers to put their clients' interests ahead of their own. Second, it implies that a registered representative of a broker-dealer is NOT a fiduciary. That's right, as a registered rep/agent/broker, you represent the firm. You owe your clients ethical, equitable behavior, but you represent the firm, bottom line.

But an adviser is a fiduciary who always has to put the client's interests first, avoiding any conflicts of interest.

Let's look at the specifics of this adopted model rule. Not sure why they had to spell out the first point to advisers, but they are simply reminding them not to recommend the purchase or sale of any security unless they have reasonable grounds to believe it's a suitable recommendation.

File that one under the DUH column and keep moving.

The second item is a little surprising to me. I would have figured the adviser needs written discretionary authority from the client before using discretionary power, but it turns out the client can give oral authorization to get the discretionary nature of the account going. The adviser then has 10 business days after the first discretionary order is placed to obtain written authorization. And, as always, time/price do NOT equal discretion.

The next item simply says that advisers should not try to induce their clients to become frantic traders, especially if the adviser is getting compensated for those transactions. So, churning is always a bad idea, and an even worse idea if the adviser is getting paid to broker the trades.

Yes, these regulators insist on taking all the fun out of the business.

The only difference I can see between items #2 and #4 would be that item #2 could be read as separating "discretionary power" into the three major aspects of a discretionary order (activity, asset, amount), whereas item #4 speaks to the overall transaction. So, item #2 says don't choose the activity, asset, or amount without proper discretionary authority, and item #4 says don't do a transaction without authority to do so.

Item #5 is basically saying that if your client's husband calls up and says his wife wants you to sell 1,000 shares of MSFT, you can only do so if the client has given her husband written trading authorization and you have that on file. Otherwise, you have to talk to your customer, the wife. Don't take orders from anybody but your client, unless the third party has been granted written third-party trading authorization.

Sometimes it's shocking that they have to spell out such obvious rules. But spell them out they do. In great, oppressive detail.

Borrowing money from clients is a practice that makes regulators real nervous. An investment adviser can only borrow money from a client if the client is a broker-dealer, an affiliate of the adviser, or a financial institution in the business of making loans (Bank, Savings & Loan, Thrift, etc.). Shocking that advisory firms would have the nerve to ask any other client to, like, spot 'em a couple bucks until payday, but, apparently, it's happened in the past and isn't supposed to happen again in the future.

Neither a borrower nor a lender be, except as prescribed by law or properly exempted/excluded statutorily, as the great Benjamin Franklin might have said if he had no interest in posterity. So, don't borrow from customers unless the customer is in the business of loaning money. And, don't lend money to a customer unless your advisory firm is in the business of making loans, or the customer is an affiliate of your advisory firm.

Item #8 really takes the fun out of being an adviser. These heavy handed regulators insist that I not lie about my qualifications, the qualifications of my employees, or the services we will provide through our contract with the client and the fees we will charge for performing those services. So, I guess now I can't tell my clients I have an MBA from the University of Chicago when, in fact, I have a BA in philosophy from the University of Illinois *at* Chicago.

Geeze, it's gettin' to where a feller can't even sneeze without violating some regulation.

Item #9 is a little tricky and, therefore, fertile ground for harvesting exam questions. If I provide a report or a recommendation to a client when, in fact, that report or recommendation was actually prepared by someone else, I have to disclose the fact and tell you who provided it. However, if I order prepared reports or use published research/statistical analyses to come up with my recommendations, that's different. No disclosure there. I'm just doing my homework to come up with a better plan for my customer.

See the difference?

Item #10 also takes all the fun out of the business by prohibiting advisers from gouging their clients.

The next item would probably produce a test question. Basically, it's just saying that if the advice being given will also lead to the advisory firm or any of its employees receiving a commission or any other compensation should the client act on the advice, that potential conflict of interest must be disclosed in writing in advance of giving/ rendering the advice. In other words, wouldn't you feel better about paying for investment advice knowing that the advice is being given by a totally objective professional, rather than someone who will make a big commission check if you take the advice? So, if the person rendering the advice stands to benefit from the transaction being recommended, that needs to be disclosed in writing ahead of time.

Item #12 is the very familiar prohibition against guarantees. Don't guarantee a specific result. Don't guarantee a profit. Don't guarantee against a loss.

Item #13 is what it is.

Item #14 is a likely testable point: don't divulge the identity, affairs, or investments of your client to anyone else without the client's permission or some sort of legal order to turn the information over to a court or the police. Might be tempting to show prospects what you've done for, say, Oprah Winfrey's account, but both Ms. Winfrey and the state securities Administrator would probably have a real problem with that.

Item #15 basically boils down to, "Be real careful what you do with client funds/ securities under custody."

Item #16 looks like a test question waiting to be written. It reminds us that all advisory contracts must be in writing and must stipulate all the terms of the contract: services provided, term of the contract, advisory fees, formula for computing the fees, the amount of prepaid fees that are refundable, whether the adviser has discretion, and that no assignment of contract can occur without client consent. That last one just means the firm can't give the client's account to a different money manager unless the client gives his/her/their consent. Wouldn't you be bummed if you called the adviser representative you've worked with for 17 years only to discover that some money manager you've never met is now handling your money?

Ouch.

Items #17 and #18 are pretty clear. Item #19 reminds us that no waivers of any provision are allowed. In other words, let's say that you and I don't like the fact that you can't compensate me as a share of capital gains, so we get an attorney to draw up a waiver that says it's okay, since we both agree that it's okay.

Nope. It's not okay.

No waivers allowed. Everybody lives by the same rules, even the ones who don't like the rules.

Item #20 seems important to me. In its legalistic, circuitous route, it points out that whether an adviser is subject to state registration, federal-only, or exempted from registration at the federal level, the firm can still get busted for fraudulent, deceptive practices by the state Administrator. Remember that. Your firm or your security might not have to be registered at the state (or even the federal) level. Big deal. The Administrator ALWAYS has the power to enforce anti-fraud rules, no matter how big you are or think you are.

Yes?

And item #21 is very typical of these detailed lists. It reminds us that this list is "not inclusive," meaning this is just *some* of the stuff we felt like talking about in THIS particular publication. It does not represent ALL of the stuff that can get you in trouble.

So be on your best behavior.

THIS IS THE ACTUAL DOCUMENT REPRINTED WITH PERMISSION FROM NASAA.
A Plain English version immediately follows.

NASAA Statement of Policy

DISHONEST OR UNETHICAL BUSINESS PRACTICES BY BROKER-DEALERS AND GENTS IN CONNECTION WITH INVESTMENT COMPANY SHARES

NASAA Broker-Dealer Sales Practices Committee

Adopted 4/27/97

Any broker dealer or agent who engages in one or more of the following practices shall be deemed to have engaged in "dishonest or unethical practices in the securities business" as used in Section 204 of the Uniform Securities Act and such conduct may constitute grounds for denial, suspension or revocation of registration or such other action authorized by statute.

A. Sales Load Communications:

1. In connection with the solicitation of investment company shares, failing to adequately disclose to a customer all sales charges, including asset based and contingent deferred sales charges, which may be imposed with respect to the purchase, retention or redemption of such shares.

2. In connection with the solicitation of investment company shares, stating or implying to a customer that the shares are sold without a commission, are "no load" or have "no sales charge" if there is associated with the purchase of the shares: (i) a front-end load; (ii) a contingent deferred sales load; (iii) a SEC Rule 12b-1 fee or a service fee if such fees in total exceeds .25% of average net fund assets per year; or (iv) in the case of closed-end investment company shares, underwriting fees, commissions or other offering expenses.

3. In connection with the solicitation of investment company shares, failing to disclose to any customer any relevant: (i) sales charge discount on the purchase of shares in dollar amounts at or above a breakpoint; or (ii) letter of intent feature, if available, which will reduce the sales charges.

4. In connection with the solicitation of investment company shares, recommending to a customer the purchase of a specific class of investment company shares in connection with a multi-class sales charge or fee arrangement without reasonable grounds to believe that the sales charge or fee arrangement associated with such class of shares is suitable and appropriate based on the customer's investment objectives, financial situation and other securities holdings, and the associated transaction or other fees.

B. Recommendations:

1. In connection with the solicitation of investment company shares, recommending to a customer the purchase of investment company shares which results in the customer simultaneously holding shares in different investment company portfolios having similar investment objectives and policies without reasonable grounds to believe that such recommendation is suitable and appropriate based on the customer's investment objectives, financial situation and other securities holdings, and any associated transaction charges or other fees.

2. In connection with the solicitation of investment company shares, recommending to a customer the liquidation or redemption of investment company shares for the purpose of purchasing shares in a different investment company portfolio having similar investment objectives and policies without reasonable grounds to believe that such recommendation is suitable and appropriate based on the customer's investment objectives, financial situation and other securities holdings and any associated transaction charges or other fees.

C. Disclosure:

1. In connection with the solicitation of investment company shares, stating or implying to a customer the fund's current yield or income without disclosing the fund's most recent average annual return, calculated in a manner prescribed in SEC Form N-1A, for one, five and ten year periods and fully explaining the difference between current yield and total return; provided, however, that if the fund's registration statement under the Securities Act of 1933 has been in effect for less than one, five, or ten years, the time during which the registration statement was in effect shall be substituted for the periods otherwise prescribed.

2. In connection with the solicitation of investment company shares, stating or implying to a customer that the investment performance of an investment company portfolio is comparable to that of a savings account, certificate of deposit or other bank deposit account without disclosing to the customer that the shares are not insured or otherwise guaranteed by the FDIC or any other government agency and the relevant differences regarding risk, guarantees, fluctuation of principal and/or return, and any other factors which are necessary to ensure that such comparisons are fair, complete and not misleading.

3. In connection with the solicitation of investment company shares, stating or implying to a customer the existence of insurance, credit quality, guarantees or similar features regarding securities held, or proposed to be held, in the investment company's portfolio

without disclosing to the customer other kinds of relevant investment risks, including but not limited to, interest rate, market, political, liquidity, or currency exchange risks, which may adversely affect investment performance and result in loss and/or fluctuation of principal notwithstanding the creditworthiness of such portfolio securities.

4. In connection with the solicitation of investment company shares, stating or implying to a customer: (i) that the purchase of such shares shortly before an ex-dividend date is advantageous to such customer unless there are specific, clearly described tax or other advantages to the customer; or (ii) that a distribution of long-term capital gains by an investment company is part of the income yield from an investment in such shares.

5. In connection with the solicitation of investment company shares, making: (i) projections of future performance; (ii) statements not warranted under existing circumstances; or (iii) statements based upon non-public information.

D. Prospectus:

In connection with the solicitation of investment company shares, the delivery of a

prospectus, in and of itself, shall not be dispositive that the broker dealer or agent provided the customer full and fair disclosure.

E. Definitions:

For the purpose of this rule the following terms shall mean:

1. "Recommend": any affirmative act or statement that endorses, solicits, requests, or commends a securities transaction to a customer or any affirmative act or statement that solicits, requests, commands, importunes or intentionally aids such person to engage in such conduct.

2. "Solicitation": any oral, written or other communication used to offer or sell investment company shares excluding any proxy statement, report to shareholders, or other disclosure document relating to a security covered under Section 18(b)(2) of the Securities Act of 1933 that is required to be and is filed with the Commission or any national securities organization registered under Section 15A of the Securities Exchange Act of 1934.

(Note: This Statement of Policy is intended to supplement, not supplant, the NASAA Statement of Policy Regarding the Dishonest or Unethical Business Practices.)

PLAIN ENGLISH VERSION

NASAA Statement of Policy:
Dishonest or Unethical Business Practices by Broker-Dealers and Agents in Connection
with Investment Company Shares
Adopted 04/27/97

As this adopted policy statement says, agents and broker-dealers need to be careful when explaining mutual funds to prospects and clients. Customers often think that their "no-load fund" doesn't charge them for distribution expenses, when, in fact, most "no-load" funds still have "12b-1 fees" that cover distribution expenses. Distribution expenses include printing, mailing, selling, and advertising. If an underwriter bears those costs, the fund has a sales charge to pay back the underwriter, plus a small profit for their trouble. If the fund covers those costs and distributes shares themselves, they usually have a 12b-1 fee to pay themselves back.

Since they both end up costing the investor money, the terms "sales charge" and "12 b-1 fee" need to be made very clear to customers.

The first item of this policy statement just reminds us to adequately disclose all front-end loads, back-end loads (contingent deferred sales charges), and 12b-1fees to customers and prospects.

The next item says that if anybody states or implies that the mutual fund shares are sold without a commission, are "no load" or have "no sales charge" when, in fact, there IS a front-end load or a contingent deferred sales charge (back-end load), that would be dishonest and/or unethical.

If the 12b-1 fee exceeds .25% (25 basis points) of average net assets, the agent can't sell the shares under the description "no load." That, of course, implies that if the 12b-1 fee is equal to or *less* than 25 basis points, they *can* get away with calling it no-load. I would still expect the agent in the test question to point out there is a 12b-1 fee explained in the prospectus, which should be understood before purchasing the shares.

Remember those wonderful selling points, such as breakpoints, rights of accumulation, combination privileges, etc.?

Well, this policy statement tells agents and their firms to make sure customers understand any breakpoints (quantity discounts) that may be available and/or any

LOI (letter of intent) features that would reduce the sales charges. Seems surprising that NASAA would have to spell that out for the industry, but, perhaps the industry has been a little too focused on closing sales rather than on disclosing sales charges.

Item number 4 states that if the agent/firm is pitching several different fund products that all involve separate sales charges, the rep/firm had better have reasonable grounds to believe that the specific class of fund shares being recommended is suitable based on the customer's investment objectives, financial situation, and other securities holdings. In other words, don't pitch it just because you're trying to put together a massive, multi-faceted mutual fund mosaic that creates all sorts of wonderful commissions for you but all sorts of nasty sales charges for your customer.

Seems fair, right?

Section B makes a similar point. If you're putting customers into several different funds—well, are they really different? Many mutual fund portfolios that might seem distinct actually hold similar securities and have similar objectives. So, why pay three different mutual fund companies three sets of sales charges and expense levels when they all hold, more or less, the same stuff?

If your customer is paying lots of extra loads/expenses to hold the same basic stuff, you'd better have reasonable grounds to believe that this is somehow suitable and appropriate.

Similarly, if you talk a customer into dumping the shares she currently owns in order to transfer the money into other portfolios that are, more or less, the same, you'd better have reasonable grounds to believe that this is suitable for the customer, and not just your wallet.

Section C starts out reminding us that "yield" is nothing more than dividend (or "income") distributions divided by the public offering price. Just like for a share of stock trading on an exchange. You take the annual dividend divided by the price paid for the security. Don't confuse this with "total return" and make sure your customer is not confused, as well. Whenever you mention "yield," you have to also mention the fund's total return over 1-, 5-, and 10-year periods (or life of fund for newer funds) as stipulated by the SEC, and you have to explain the difference between yield and total return to the customer.

An agent might mention that a particular fund had a performance comparable to a savings account, CD, or other bank deposit account without disclosing that the shares aren't guaranteed/insured the way the bank products are. That would be sort of like saying that your friend once drove a golf ball farther than Tiger Woods without also disclosing that the ball ended up on the wrong fairway, your friend ended up taking a double bogie on the hole and shot a 57 on the back nine.

Right?

Gotta tell the whole story if you're going to compare your buddy to Tiger Woods, or an uninsured mutual fund product to a totally insured/secure bank deposit.

Even if the mutual fund you're pitching holds nothing but insured or guaranteed securities, you still have to point out other risks. A T-bond has no default risk, because the government will pay you back. But, it still retains interest-rate risk. Rates up—price down, end of story. In fact, a 30-year T-bond has much more of this risk than, say, a 10-year corporate bond. Some of these products could also have foreign currency exchange risk, political risk, or liquidity risk. If so, you have to point that out, in addition to the "insured" or "guaranteed credit quality" feature.

You already know that the regulators hate the practice of "selling dividends" and the next item reminds you not to entice a customer to buy a fund just because it's about to pay a dividend. Remember, even with the new tax rates, customers still get taxed on the dividend and watch the share price drop right after getting the dividend. So, there would have to be a clearly described tax or other advantage to making the purchase at this time. Also, the item reminds you to remind the customer that capital gains distributions are NOT part of income yield. Income yield equals dividends divided by POP.

And never, never, ever give a mutual fund projection. "Past performance does not guarantee future results," pretty well sums up that idea. Also, don't make any statements based on material, non-public information or statements not warranted under existing circumstances. An example of the latter would be a statement like, "I don't know, I just have a real strong feeling that this fund is going to outperform the other 800 aggressive growth funds in its peer group." First, that would be a projection, especially if you attached a number to it. And, second, it's a statement not warranted because you have no flippin' idea what's going to happen until it happens.

And, then, just to make sure everybody's real clear on the language they're using, NASAA defines the terms "recommend" and "solicitation" as follows:

1. "Recommend": any affirmative act or statement that endorses, solicits, requests, or commends a securities transaction to a customer or any affirmative act or statement that solicits, requests, commands, importunes or intentionally aids such person to engage in such conduct.

2. "Solicitation": any oral, written or other communication used to offer or sell investment company shares excluding any proxy statement, report to shareholders, or other disclosure document relating to a security covered under Section 18(b)(2) of the Securities Act of 1933 that is required to be and is filed with the commission or

any national securities organization registered under Section 15A of the Securities Exchange Act of 1934.

Well, that sure clears things up, huh? Aren't you glad you paid the price of this material so you don't have to translate all the legalese yourself?

In case you care—and I'm not sure that you should—the definition of "recommend" should cover just about anything that could possibly be construed as pushing a customer toward buying an investment company product. Not sure how often you'll be "importuning" your customers; I have a feeling your boss would probably prefer that you go ahead and actually sell something, but I'll leave that up to your firm.

The definition of "solicitation" starts out real clear, then turns into the usual soliloquy that excludes everybody that needs excluding from the otherwise simple definition. "Any oral, written or other communication used to offer or sell investment company shares," could not have been clearer. Unfortunately, they then have to make sure everybody understands they're not talking about proxies, shareholder reports, or disclosure documents.

Whew! Thank God you know that, huh?

THIS IS THE ACTUAL DOCUMENT REPRRINTED WITH PERMISSION FROM NASAA.
A plain English version follows.

MODEL RULES FOR SALES OF SECURITIES AT FINANCIAL INSTITUTIONS

Adopted 10/6/98

(A) Applicability

These rules apply exclusively to broker-dealer services conducted by broker-dealers on the premises of a financial institution where retail deposits are taken.

These rules do not alter or abrogate a broker-dealer's obligations to comply with other applicable laws, rules, or regulations that may govern the operations of broker-dealers and their agents, including but not limited to, supervisory obligations. These rules do not apply to broker-dealer services provided to non-retail customers.

(B) Definitions

For purposes of these rules, the following terms have the meanings indicated:

(1) "Financial institution" means federal and state-chartered banks, savings and loan associations, savings banks, credit unions, and the service corporations of such institutions located in [name of state].2

(2) "Networking arrangement" means a contractual or other arrangement between a broker-dealer and a financial institution pursuant to which the broker-dealer conducts broker-dealer services on the premises of such financial institution where retail deposits are taken.

(3) "Broker-dealer services" means the investment banking or securities business as defined in paragraph (p) of Article I of the By-Laws of the National Association of Securities Dealers, Inc.

(C) Standards For Broker-Dealer Conduct

No broker-dealer shall conduct broker-dealer services on the premises of a financial institution where retail deposits are taken unless the broker-dealer complies initially and continuously with the following requirements:

(1) Setting

Wherever practical, broker-dealer services shall be conducted in a physical location distinct from the area in which the financial institution's retail deposits are taken. In those situations where there is insufficient space to allow separate areas, the broker-dealer has a heightened responsibility to distinguish its services from those of the financial institution. In all situations, the broker-dealer shall identify its services in a manner that clearly distinguishes those services from the financial institution's retail deposit-taking activities. The broker-dealer's name

1 "Non-retail customer" may be replaced with "institutional investor" if defined in state law.

2 Existing state law definition of "financial institution" may be used instead. shall be clearly displayed in the area in which the broker-dealer conducts its services.

(2) Networking Arrangements and Program Management

Networking arrangements shall be governed by a written agreement that sets forth the responsibilities of the parties and the compensation arrangements. Networking arrangements must provide that supervisory personnel of the broker-dealer and representatives of state securities authorities, where authorized by state law, will be permitted access to the financial institution's premises where the broker-dealer conducts broker-dealer services in order to inspect the books and records and other relevant information maintained by the broker-dealer with respect to its brokerdealer services. Management of the broker-dealer shall be responsible for ensuring that the networking arrangement clearly outlines the duties and responsibilities of all parties, including those of financial institution personnel.

(3) Customer Disclosure And Written Acknowledgment

(a) At or prior to the time that a customer's securities brokerage account is opened by a broker-dealer on the premises of a financial institution where retail deposits are taken, the broker-dealer shall:

(i) Disclose, orally and in writing, that the securities products purchased or sold in a transaction with the broker-dealer:

(A) Are not insured by the Federal Deposit Insurance Corporation ("FDIC");3

(B) Are not deposits or other obligations of the financial institution and are not guaranteed by the financial institution;

and

(C) Are subject to investment risks, including possible loss of the principal invested.

(ii) Make reasonable efforts to obtain from each customer during the account opening process a written acknowledgment of the disclosures required by paragraph (C)(3)(a)(i).

(b) If broker-dealer services include any written or oral representations concerning insurance coverage, other than FDIC insurance coverage, then clear and accurate written or oral explanations of the coverage must also be provided to the customers when such representations are first made.

(4) Communications With The Public

(a) (i) All of the broker-dealer's confirmations and account statements must indicate clearly that the broker-dealer services are provided by the brokerdealer.

(ii) Advertisements and sales literature that announce the location of a financial institution where broker-dealer services are provided by the broker-dealer, or that are distributed by the broker-dealer on the

3 "FDIC" should be replaced with alternate insurance program, e.g. NCUA, is applicable. Also, inapplicability of any state deposit insurance program should be disclosed. premises of a financial institution, must disclose that securities products: are not insured by the FDIC; are not deposits or other obligations of the financial institution and are not guaranteed by the financial institution; and are subject to investment risks, including possible loss of the principal invested. The shorter, logo format described in paragraph (C) (4) (b) (i) may be used to provide these disclosures.

(iii) Recommendations by a broker-dealer concerning non-deposit investment products with a name similar to that of a financial institution must only occur pursuant to policies and procedures reasonably designed to minimize risk of customer confusion.

(b) (i) The following shorter, logo format disclosures may be used by a broker-dealer in advertisements and sales literature, including material published, or designed for use, in radio or television broadcasts, Automated Teller Machine ("ATM") screens, billboards, signs, posters and brochures, to comply with the requirements of paragraph (C) (4) (a) (ii), provided that such disclosures are displayed in a conspicuous manner:

(a) Not FDIC Insured

(b) No Bank Guarantee

(c) May Lose Value

(ii) As long as the omission of the disclosures required by paragraph

(C) (4) (a) (ii) Would not cause the advertisement or sales literature to be misleading in light of the context in which the material is presented, such disclosures are not required with respect to messages contained in:

(a) Radio broadcasts of 30 seconds or less;

(b) Electronic signs, including billboard-type signs that are electronic, time, and temperature signs and ticker tape signs, but excluding messages contained in such media as television, on-line computer services, or ATMs; and

(c) Signs, such as banners and posters, when used only as location indicators.

(5) Notification Of Termination

The broker-dealer must promptly notify the financial institution if any agent of the broker-dealer who is employed by the financial institution is terminated for cause by the broker-dealer.

PLAIN ENGLISH VERSION

NASAA Adopted Model Rule: Sales of Securities at Financial Institutions
Adopted 10/06/98

Used to be that banks were prohibited from acting as broker-dealers. The Glass-Steagall Act made sure that banks remained a safe place to deposit federally insured money while broker-dealers could offer some relatively safe havens as well as some risky (or extremely risky) places to invest. Well, major chunks of Glass-Steagall were recently repealed, so now you do see broker-dealers acting on the premises of banks. For some, this is probably hard to get used to, especially people who grew up during the Great Depression. After all those bank failures that caused so much misery in the 1930's, some folks are probably surprised to see banks pushing mutual funds and variable annuities, neither of which are insured by the FDIC.

Oh well. The times they are a' changin'.

So, the regulators have to lay down some rules for accommodating this sudden push into brave, new territory. As NASAA's Adopted Model Rule makes clear, great care must be taken to help customers separate the important differences between banks and broker-dealers whenever broker-dealers operate at the same location where retail deposits are taken. These rules apply to more than just "banks," too. The Adopted Model Rule uses the term "financial institution," in order to catch all the following: federal and state-chartered banks, savings & loan associations, savings banks, credit unions, and the service corporations of such institutions. So, if I saw a choice that read something like "any financial institution regulated by the Federal Reserve Board," I'd be mighty tempted to associate that with this.

The rule also states that it applies to broker-dealers who deal with retail customers. If the B/D only deals with institutional clients, we don't need to go to all this trouble of separating bank from broker-dealer in everything we say and do at the bank where the broker-dealer has set up shop. As usual, the "little guy" (retail) needs a higher level of protection than the "big guy" (institutional investor, i.e. insurance company, mutual fund, pension fund) does.

Broker-dealer services include "investment banking and securities business as defined in paragraph (p) of Article I of the By-Laws of the National Association of Securities Dealers, Inc." If you want to go read the By-Laws, it might be worth your time. You might want to read those anyway before hooking up with an NASD firm.

But, I'm not going to go there right now. We're not absolutely sure you'll see any questions relating to any of the stuff in this adopted model rule. Trouble is, you *could* see questions on it, and that's why we have to be ready.

Just in case. And the topic seems very timely about now, as broker-dealers and banks get harder and harder to distinguish, especially for the average or "retail" investor.

So, let's get the basics.

Section C "Standards for Broker-Dealer Conduct" makes it clear that broker-dealers need to make it clear to customers that the broker-dealer is a whole nuther ballgame from the bank. Wherever possible, the broker-dealer business should be conducted in a physical location distinct from the area in which the financial institution takes retail deposits. And, in those cases where that physical distinction is impractical, there is a heightened responsibility for the broker-dealer to make it real clear to the customer that she has strayed far from the world of FDIC-insured deposits, even if it feels as if she has only crossed the lobby and veered left at the coffee kiosk. In all cases, these broker-dealers set up on the premises of financial institutions need to identify their services in a manner that clearly distinguishes those services from the financial institution's retail deposit-taking activities. And, the broker-dealer's name must be displayed in the area in which they conduct business.

Have you been to a bank lately? Have you noticed all the fine print under the advertisements for IRA's, mutual funds, variable annuities, etc.? These materials always point out that, unlike a bank deposit or CD, this product is not FDIC-insured and you could, like, lose all your money on this one. This model rule says that the broker-dealer, either before or at the time of opening the account, must disclose to the customer orally AND in writing that the securities products purchased or sold through the broker-dealer:

- are not insured by the FDIC
- are not deposits or obligations of the financial institution, and are not guaranteed by the financial institution
- are subject to investment risk, including the possibility of losing the whole ball of wax, which they, instead, call "possible loss of the principal invested"

The broker-dealer must also make a reasonable effort to get the customer to sign something attesting to the fact that he has now had the beejeezus sufficiently scared out of him but chooses to risk this whole "possible loss of the principal invested" thing anyway in an effort to invest for his non-FDIC-insured, non-government-guaranteed future.

As long as it is displayed in a conspicuous (easily noticed) way, the model rule also allows the following shorter "logo format" versions of these dire warnings:

- Not FDIC Insured
- No Bank Guarantee
- May Lose Value

You may have seen those three bullet points recently on an advertisement for securities products at your local branch. If not, next time you're waiting in line for the next available teller, see if you can find any of this language throughout the lobby.

Section C-4 talks about written communications with customers and prospects, starting with trade confirmations and account statements. These communications must always make it clear that it's the broker-dealer (not the financial institution) that provides these services. Any advertisements or sales literature that announces the location of the financial institution where the broker-dealer operates must also include either the longer or "shorter, logo format" disclosures about the non-FDIC-insured, might-lose-your-shirt nature of securities sold by a broker-dealer.

And, when this rule discusses sales literature and advertising materials, it casts a very wide net. As the rule states, this includes: material published, or designed for use, in radio or television broadcasts, Automated Teller Machine (ATM) screens, billboards, signs, posters, and brochures. Then, to keep things nice and simple, they do the usual exclusion dance. The rule states that, "As long as the omission of the disclosures would not cause the advertisement to be misleading . . . such disclosures are *not* required with respect to messages contained in:

(a) radio broadcasts of 30 seconds or less
(b) electronic signs, including billboard-type signs that are electronic, time, and temperature signs and ticker tape signs, but excluding messages contained in such media as television, on-line computer services, or ATM's; and
(c) signs, such as banners and posters, when used only as location indicators

Did you enjoy point (b)'s exclusion within the exclusion?
Gives you a whole new respect for attorneys, doesn't it?
Anyway, I really can't see the Series 63 expecting you to know all that detail, unless, of course, it does.

The next section (C- 5) just tells broker-dealers to promptly notify the financial institution if the broker-dealer for cause terminates one of the folks working for both entities. May you never actually discover what "for cause" means. It means you screwed up big-time.

Finally, this situation where a broker-dealer operates on the premises of a financial institution where retail deposits are taken is called a "networking arrangement." Not surprisingly and just like an investment advisory contract, these arrangements must be governed by a detailed, written contract that sets forth the responsibilities of both parties and the compensation arrangements. The contract must also make clear that supervisors of the broker-dealer as well as state securities regulators will be permitted access to the financial institution's premises where the broker-dealer conducts broker-dealer services in order to inspect the books and records and other relevant information. It is ultimately the responsibility of the broker-dealer's management to make sure that the responsibilities of both parties (B/D and financial institution) are made clear to all parties, including financial institution personnel.

There. Wasn't that fun?

EXERCISES

EXERCISE: ONCE MORE, IN ENGLISH!

One of the big challenges of reading securities law and taking the Series 63 exam is that the language used seems almost like a foreign tongue. Let's call it "Legalese." It's definitely English, but the rhythm is bad, the words are bizarre, and there are way too many negative words all in a row. After all, nobody likes to read a passage like, "An agent unknowingly sold an unregistered, non-exempt security to a non-accredited investor through an unsolicited order."

Huh?

Remember, time is a big factor on the Series 63. There are 65 questions and 75 minutes. Do the math—it's an evil equation.

If it takes forty seconds just to figure out what the question is asking, you will find yourself frustrated and falling behind. So, it might be a good idea to sharpen your translation skills. It might even be fun. *Big* fun.

DIRECTIONS: TAKE THE FOLLOWING PHRASES AND <u>REWRITE THEM IN YOUR OWN WORDS</u>. WHAT ARE THEY *REALLY* SAYING? SEE IF YOU CAN SIMPLIFY AND DE-CODE THE FOLLOWING:

1. It is not unlawful

2. None of the following activities are prohibited except

3. An agent unwittingly omitted an immaterial fact.

4. The security is effective concurrently with federal-level effectiveness provided no Administrative order to intervene is pending.

5. It would not be unsuitable for a risk-averse investor to not purchase penny stocks.

6. None of the following activities are unethical except

7. The Administrator may summarily suspend a pending registration.

8. Securities offered by qualification or coordination may be placed in escrow and proceeds impounded until issuer receives specified amount.

9. An isolated non-issuer transaction in outstanding securities

10. Unsolicited non-issuer order

11. An unregistered non-exempt security

12. The Administrator may establish minimum capital requirement not to exceed that required under SEC Act of 1934.

13. The definition of broker-dealer does not include a person with no office in the state who sells securities to individuals not residents of the state.

14. Represent a non-exempt issuer in non-exempt securities

15. Broker-dealer with incidental advisory services with no special compensation

16. Subject of adjudication

17. Has been enjoined by a court

18. It is unlawful for any person in connection with the offer, sale, or purchase of any security to employ any device, scheme, or artifice to defraud.

19. It is unlawful for any person in connection with the offer, sale, or purchase of any security to make any untrue statement of material fact or omit a material fact.

20. Penalties and sanctions for violations include administrative proceedings, judicial injunctions, and criminal or civil prosecutions.

21. In the absence of a rule by the Administrator prohibiting custody

22. None of the following activities are acceptable except

23. It is unlawful for an adviser to be compensated on the basis of a share of capital gains or appreciation.

24. An Investment Adviser may only act as a principal for its own account with disclosure to and consent of client.

25. Failure to disclose legal or regulatory action against adviser material to evaluation of adviser's integrity or ability to meet contractual commitments is prohibited.

DIRECTIONS: DEFINE THE FOLLOWING VOCABULARY WORDS

1. Exempt

2. Non-exempt

3. Contumacy

4. Contempt

5. Issuer

6. Offer

7. Sale/sell

8. Injunction

9. Enjoin

10. Subpoena

11. Non-punitive termination

12. Adjudication of mental incompetence

13. Aggrieved party

14. Rescission

15. Rescind

16. Convey for value a security

17. Material

18. Immaterial

19. Fiduciary

20. Effect, as in "to *effect* a transaction"

21. Render, as in "to render advice regarding securities"

22. Risk-averse

23. Insolvent

24. Defraud

25. Consent to service of process

26. Person

27. Broker-dealer

28. Agent

29. Investment adviser

30. Investment adviser representative

31. Federal covered security

32. Federal covered investment adviser

33. Impoundment of proceeds

34. Prospectus

35. Preliminary prospectus

36. Private placement

37. Market manipulation

38. Confirmation

39. Settlement

ANSWERS

1. **It is not unlawful**

   It is lawful. Or: It is okay.

2. **None of the following activities are prohibited except**

   Which of the following activities are prohibited?

3. **An agent unwittingly omitted an immaterial fact**

   An agent did not tell the customer a fact that was unimportant.

   Note: the "unwittingly" is almost meaningless in this case, just another negative word designed to confuse you. Don't let it.

4. **The security is effective concurrently with federal-level effectiveness provided no Administrative order to intervene is pending.**

   The security's effective date at the state level is the same as the SEC effective date, unless the Administrator intervenes.

   Note: concurrently, simultaneously both mean "at same time as"

5. **It would not be unsuitable for a risk-averse investor to not purchase penny stocks.**

   It would be suitable for an investor who hates risk to avoid penny stocks.

   Note: risk-averse means "opposed to risk." Risk-averse investors buy government bonds, primarily. Penny stocks are high-risk.

6. **None of the following activities are unethical except**

   Which of the following activities are unethical?

7. **The Administrator may summarily suspend a pending registration.**

   If the registration has not been granted yet (pending), the Administrator may suspend it.

   Note: unlike deny/revoke/suspend, this order may be entered even before the applicant gets a chance to request a hearing.

8. **Securities offered by qualification or coordination may be placed in escrow and proceeds impounded until issuer receives specified amount.**

   The Administrator may require the issuer to establish an escrow account where the proceeds from the sales of securities will be impounded (not released to issuer) until the issuer/underwriters have sold the specified amount of money.

9. **An isolated non-issuer transaction in outstanding securities**

   A rare or isolated transaction on the secondary market (not for benefit of issuer).

10. **Unsolicited non-issuer order**

    A transaction on the secondary market requested by the customer.

11. **An unregistered non-exempt security**

    A security that should be registered but has not been.

12. **The Administrator may establish minimum capital requirement not to exceed that required under SEC Act of 1934.**

    The Administrator may set minimum capital requirements that are never higher than those required at the federal/SEC level.

13. **The definition of broker-dealer does not include a person with no office in the state who sells securities to individuals not residents of the state.**

    A broker-dealer registered in another state is not defined as a broker-dealer in this state if they have no office here and deal with people here 30 days or less.

14. **Represent a non-exempt issuer in non-exempt securities**

    Represent an issuer with no exemption selling securities with no exemption

    Note: this individual would be defined as an agent and would have to register. Why? Neither the issuer nor the security qualify for special treatment.

15. Broker-dealer with incidental advisory services with no special compensation

Broker-dealer who does not provide regular advice for a fee.

Note: this firm is excluded from the definition of "investment advisor."

16. Subject of adjudication

Has gone through a court (ju̲d̲ge/adju̲d̲ication) process and has been judged.

17. Has been enjoined by a court

Has been hit with an injunction by a court

Note: that means the person has been prevented from doing something by a court of law. Enjoin = verb form. Injunction = noun form.

18. It is unlawful for any person in connection with the offer, sale, or purchase of any security to employ any device, scheme, or artifice to defraud.

It is unlawful to do anything deceptive when offering, selling, or purchasing securities.

Note: doesn't matter if the securities are exempt or non-exempt.

19. It is unlawful for any person in connection with the offer, sale, or purchase of any security to make any untrue statement of material fact or omit a material fact.

It is unlawful for anyone to lie about material facts or omit material facts when offering, selling, or buying securities.

Note: this would constitute fraud, deceit

20. Penalties and sanctions for violations include administrative proceedings, judicial injunctions, and criminal or civil prosecutions.

Violating the USA can lead to hearings with the Administrator, court orders preventing certain activities, and even criminal prosecutions leading to fines and/or jail time, or big monetary penalties awarded in civil court.

21. In the absence of a rule by the Administrator prohibiting custody

If the Administrator has no rule against custody

22. None of the following activities are acceptable except

Which of the following activities are okay/acceptable?

23. It is unlawful for an adviser to be compensated on the basis of a share of capital gains or appreciation.

Investment advisers may NOT be paid for capital gains or increases in market prices of securities.

Note: they either charge an hourly rate for their consulting, or they manage money and charge a fee that is a % of the assets being managed.

24. An Investment Adviser may only act as a principal for its own account with disclosure to and consent of client.

An investment advisory firm can buy securities from a client for their inventory or sell securities out of their inventory to a client only if they disclose they are doing so and only after the customer says it's okay.

Note: otherwise, advisers might have a conflict of interest. If they want to get rid of a stock nobody else seems to want, they might find an easy mark in their customer, whom they are supposed to be looking out for.

25. Failure to disclose legal or regulatory action against adviser material to evaluation of adviser's integrity or ability to meet contractual commitments is prohibited.

Investment advisers must disclose to their prospects and clients any legal or regulatory problems if the problems are material to evaluating the firm's integrity or ability to do a good job for the client.

DEFINITION ANSWERS

1. **Exempt:** not subject to; rules do not apply to

2. **Non-exempt:** has no exemption; rules <u>do</u> apply to

3. **Contumacy:** disregarding an Administrator's order

4. **Contempt:** violating a court order

5. **Issuer:** anyone who issues or proposes to issue a security

6. **Offer:** an attempt to sell, or the attempt to get someone to make an offer to buy something

7. **Sale/sell:** a "contract" to dispose of a security for "value" (money, or any other economic benefit)

8. **Injunction:** court order to prevent a person from doing something

9. **Enjoin:** to issue an injunction

10. **Subpoena:** a court order or Administrative order to appear at a hearing/ trial

11. **Non-punitive termination:** leaving a place of employment because you want to—not because you got in trouble

12. **Adjudication of mental incompetence:** a court determines that a person is not competent mentally to make important decisions

13. **Aggrieved party:** the person who has suffered grief over another person's alleged misdeeds

14. **Rescission:** the act of rescinding, the act of "undoing" a transaction

15. **Rescind:** to undo a transaction; the seller buys it back plus interest, less any income received from the security by the owner

16. **Convey for value a security:** transfer a security for money or any other economic benefit

17. Material: important, relevant

18. Immaterial: not important, irrelevant

19. Fiduciary: a person looking out for the benefit of another person

20. Effect, as in "to *effect* a transaction": to complete

21. Render, as in "to render advice regarding securities": to make and deliver

22. Risk-averse: hates risk

23. Insolvent: more liabilities than assets to pay 'em off with

24. Defraud: to deceive for financial gain

25. Consent to service of process: a form that gives the Administrator the power to receive court papers on behalf of the person filing the consent

26. Person: not dead, a minor, or mentally incompetent; a legal entity

27. Broker-dealer: a firm (sometimes an individual) in the business of completing transactions for others or for its own account.

28. Agent: individual representing either a broker-dealer or a non-exempt issuer

29. Investment adviser: person (sometimes an individual) who charges a fee for providing investment advice as an integral part of their business

30. Investment adviser representative: individual who represents an investment advisory firm by managing money, making recommendations, selling the services of the firm, or supervising anyone doing any of those advisory-type things.

31. Federal covered security: a security not subject to the state's requirements for filing of advertising materials and registration.

32. Federal covered adviser: an adviser with not less than $25,000,000 of assets under management, or anyone (even with an office in the state) who advises a registered investment company, or whose sole clients are investment companies or insurance companies. Note that federal covered

advisers still pay fees, provide notice, and file a consent to service of process with the state. But they're really under federal/SEC jurisdiction.

32. Impoundment of proceeds: establishing an escrow account where proceeds from the offering of securities are impounded/not released to the issuer by the Administrator until the specified amount of money has been raised. Note that if the amount of money raised is insufficient, the proceeds (plus a pro rata share of the interest) goes to the investors, not the issuer or underwriters.

33. Prospectus: a disclosure document that provides relevant, important, *material* facts about a security to a buyer

34. Preliminary prospectus: AKA "red herring". This is the prospectus before it's all completed. Doesn't have the final public offering price (POP) or the release date, because those haven't been determined yet.

35. Private placement: unregistered securities sold through an exemption to the Act of 1933. Securities are placed primarily in the hands of sophisticated investors, including officers and directors of the issuer, institutional buyers (mutual funds, insurance companies, pension funds), or accredited investors.

36. Market manipulation: an extremely exciting activity that will get you in more trouble than you bargained for. Includes words like: *pegging, capping, painting the tape, wash sales, matched purchases*

37. Confirmation: what it sounds like, a document confirming a transaction. These must be delivered to customers no later than settlement. For a new issue, the prospectus must be delivered with or before confirmation.

38. Settlement: when the buyer of a security is officially recognized as the owner by the transfer agent. T + 3 for most securities, T + 1 for Treasury securities.

EXERCISE: THE USUAL SUSPECTS

Defining persons is a BIG part of this exam. Not only must you define the persons to answer certain questions, but also you often need to understand what these terms mean just to understand what the heck the question is asking.

So this next exercise is designed to help you sharpen your definition skills. You really aren't ready for the Series 63 until your are confident that you can define the big four players:

- broker-dealer
- agent
- investment adviser
- investment adviser representative

So, let's get ready.

THE USUAL SUSPECTS

DIRECTIONS: look at the following line-ups very carefully. Your accurate identification of these entities is crucial. After reading the facts, determine which of the four suspects is, in fact, the one we're looking for. The other three have to be released from scrutiny.

For now.

1. **Which one of the suspects below is defined as an** agent?

#1   #2   #3   #4

 #1 – represents General Electric in the sale of commercial paper to a mutual fund with no special compensation paid for the sales
 #2 – represents the Municipal Government of Mount Matasky, Montana in the sale of general obligation bonds to several large pension funds in Minnesota
 #3 – represents Johnson & Doolin Broker-Dealership in the sale of commercial paper to institutional investors
 #4 – represents General Electric in selling GE stock to GE employees for which no commission is paid

2. **Which of the following suspects is most likely defined as an** investment adviser representative?

#1   #2   #3   #4

 #1 – an investment adviser (sole proprietorship) registered in the state, providing regular advice to pension funds for a fee
 #2 – an individual hired by a federal covered adviser primarily for administrative tasks and obvious ability to entertain clients at company functions
 #3 – individual hired, against all odds, to sell the services of an investment adviser
 #4 – an investment adviser not registered in the state, providing advice on Treasury securities not registered in the state

3. Which of the following four suspects must register as an investment adviser in the state of Wisconsin?

M&N

Registered in IL

Does business with 13 insurance companies in WI.

QRZ

Registered in IL

Does business with 9 pension funds in WI

LTZ, Ltd.

Registered in IL

Does business with 25 mutual funds in WI.

Directs faxes to 4 non-institutional investors in WI.

Z & T

Registered in IL

Directs faxes to 7 non-institutional clients in WI over past 12 months.

4. Which of the following persons is defined as an investment adviser in the state of Tennessee?

D&R

Insurance Company Registered in IL

QRZ

Insurance Company Registered in TN

Gomez & Gomez

Law firm in TN

Develops estate plans

Provides advice incidental to law practice.

Jones & Barney

Law firm in TN

Provides advice as integral component of law practice.

5. Which of the following investment advisers has committed a prohibited act?

D&R

Took custody of customer funds in the absence of a rule prohibiting custody, informing the Adviser in writing.

QRZ

Omitted immaterial information while delivering investment advice for a fee.

Gomez & Gomez

Frequently assigns customer contracts to different adviser reps with express written consent of clients.

Jones & Barney

Frequently acts as principal for own account in recommending securities without disclosure and consent.

6. **Which of the following suspects would most likely end up having their registration as a broker-dealer denied, suspended, or revoked?**

D&R
Was convicted of a misdemeanor involving securities 9 years ago and omits this fact on application for registration.

TRY, Inc.
Aggressively trades proprietary account while recommending lower-beta, slower-growth investments to retail customers.

Gomez & Gomez
Has three registered principals, but none has an MBA or CFA.

Ross & Ross
Was convicted of a non-securities related misdemeanor in past 10 years and discloses this fact on application for registration.

6. **Which of the following securities is subject to state-level registration?**

DXL
Common Stock Listed on NYSE

ALDG
Unlisted, OTC stock. Quoted regularly on NASDAQ

XTXL
OTC Bulletin Board-traded common stock

G.O.
General Obligation bond of the State of California

7. **Three of the following suspects have been planted in the line-up to serve as decoys. Only one of them is actually a security. Which one is it?**

Annuity paying a guaranteed rate of return

Put option on a grain futures contract

Grain futures contract

Term-Life Insurance Policy

8. **All of the following are securities, except for one impostor. Which one is not actually a security?**

| Whiskey Warehouse Receipt | 10% interest in a racehorse | Commercial Paper | Fixed Annuity |

9. **All of the following agents have committed prohibited acts except which one?**

#1 #2 #3 #4

#1 – accepted an order for an unregistered, non-exempt security from a non-discretionary customer by way of an individual without third-party trading authorization

#2 – indicated on a recent client letter that he was approved by the Administrator for performing technical and fundamental analysis

#3 – failed to recommend municipal securities to a low-income investor with capital appreciation as an investment objective

#4 – made a blanket recommendation to 73 different clients to buy a low-priced, thinly traded biotechnology stock

ANSWERS

1. Suspect #3 is the only agent in this lineup. #3 represents a broker-dealer. #1 represents an issuer selling exempt securities (commercial paper). #2 represents an exempt issuer (municipal issuer). And, #4 represents an issuer in an exempt transaction—if he got commissions, the transaction would lose the exemption.

2. Suspect #3 is an individual—investment adviser representatives are always individuals. #1 is eliminated because the adviser is the not the adviser representative, just like the Cubs are not Sammy Sosa—one is the overall entity; one plays for that entity. Individuals hired for clerical/ministerial work are not consider adviser representatives. Adviser representatives manage money, determine recommendations, sell the services of the firm, or supervise those who do any of that stuff.

3. #4, Z&T is defined as an investment adviser in Wisconsin because they're over the "de minimus" exemption of 5 non-institutional investors. They could have dealt with all the institutions they wanted, but they can only direct communications to 5 or fewer non-accredited/non-institutional investors.

4. # 4, Jones & Barney is a firm that must register as an investment adviser because their advice is an integral component of their practice. Insurance companies are not investment advisers; rather, they are defined as *insurance companies*. Note that the other law firm provides advice that is incidental/not integral to their practice. That's how a law firm maintains their exemption—but if the advice becomes an integral component, they lose they exemption and must register as investment advisers.

5. #4, Jones & Barney may not act as a principal for its own account without client consent and full disclosure of the potential conflict of interest. Omitting material information is bad; omitting IM-material information is a good thing. It leaves out the irrelevant stuff. Contracts may be assigned to different adviser representatives, as long as client's give their consent. #1, D&R would have had their registration denied, revoked, or suspended because of the securities-related misdemeanor that occurred in the past 10 years—omitting that fact from their registration statement might seem convenient, but will get them into even bigger trouble. TRY can aggressively trade their own account and would be expected to recommend lower risk securities to most—if not all—clients. CFA and MBA are nice credentials, but not legal requirements.

6. #3, XTXL will have to register at the state level because it does not qualify for a "blue chip" or "manual" exemption. Listed and NASDAQ stocks register at the federal level. They might provide a "notice filing" to the state, but that's just a heads up to the Administrator—they're really on the SEC's turf.

7. #2, options on futures ARE securities, even though the underlying futures/commodities are not. Fixed annuities and life insurance with fixed/guaranteed payments are NOT securities.

8. #4, remember that annuities and insurance that pays a fixed/guaranteed return are NOT securities. Commercial paper might be "exempt" from registration, but it is still a security. An exempt security is still a security; it just has different registration requirements.

9. #3, the words "failed to recommend" somehow make it sound like something wrong happened; it didn't. Low-income investors with capital appreciation as objectives should not be talked into municipal bonds. Rather, they should be considering common stock or mutual funds with growth/capital appreciation as an objective. Now that we're in the right category, we would determine risk. If the customer has a large appetite for risk, we'll recommend things like small cap, biotechnology, overseas opportunity, or aggressive growth funds. If their risk tolerance is much lower, we can recommend blue chip stock funds. And, of course, the biggest part of your exam will involve spotting unethical, deceptive, fraudulent, or otherwise prohibited business practices by these broker-dealers, agents, investment advisers and IA reps that you have now diligently defined.

Exercise: What's Wrong with That?

And, of course, the biggest part of your exam will involve spotting unethical, deceptive, fraudulent, or otherwise prohibited business practices by these broker-dealers, agents, investment advisers and IA reps that you have now diligently defined.

Most of the bad stuff seems obvious, but you can't always rely on your gut. You really need to become sort of an expert on spotting the no-no's in this business.

Ready?

DIRECTIONS: read the following passages and highlight all the instances of unethical, prohibited practices. After you've marked all the violations make a list and briefly explain why they are considered violations.

1. RYAN REYNOLDS

Ryan Reynolds has been having a tough time on the new job. All the other representatives at the firm have been making nice commissions, while Ryan is still struggling to build up his book of business. Since it seems obvious he won't be pulling in many new clients for a while, Ryan decides to call his existing clients and make something happen.

The first customer he contacts is skeptical about buying any securities at this point. In order to allay the customer's fear, Ryan offers to go partners on a purchase of 1,000 shares of a hot biotech stock. This way if the stock goes up, he and the customer will sell and split the profits. And, if the stock goes down, they'll sell it at a loss and split that for tax purposes.

The customer still isn't sure.

"Look," Ryan assures him, "you can't lose on this stock. I heard they were maybe going to be bought out pretty soon."

"By who?" the customer asks.

"I don't know. I'm just telling you what I heard, and, please, don't repeat it, okay?"

"What's their earnings look like, Ryan?"

"Pretty strong, actually."

"So, they're making money, then?"

"Absolutely."

What Ryan actually means is that the company has been trimming their losses impressively. The company lost $5 million two years ago and only $1.5 million the most recent quarter.

"Well," the customer says, "you know I only buy stocks with positive earnings."

"Oh, I know," Ryan says. "That's why I think you should be into this one. Let me put you into 10,000 shares this morning. What do you say?"

"You know I don't like to buy more than a round lot first time out."

"Yeah, but, this stock is only trading at three bucks a share."

"Three bucks? I don't buy penny stocks."

"It's not a penny stock—they're listed."

Ryan is pretty sure they're listed.

What, if anything, did Ryan do wrong today?

2. DENISE DENKO

Denise Denko is in business for herself as an investment adviser. Her clients and she like the "old-fashioned" way of doing business, which is why all advisory contracts with her customers are verbal agreements, sealed with a handshake. To align her interests with theirs Denise charges no fee unless her clients' portfolios gain more than the S & P 500 index. She also takes 10% of any capital gains realized and 5% of any capital appreciation.

On her letterhead, Denise indicates that she has been approved by the Administrator to perform both technical and fundamental analysis. Denise is also an agent with a broker-dealership, which she uses to place all customer trades. Since her clients implicitly trust her judgment, Denise sees no reason to inform them of this arrangement. While the broker-dealership does not charge the lowest commissions available to her clients, it does charge what she considers a fair and reasonable commission and/or markup.

What, if anything, is Denise doing that may be considered unethical?

3. Ryan Reynolds

Ryan Reynolds receives an angry letter from a customer upset that Ryan did not sell the customer's 500 shares of Enron as instructed. Ryan knows that his branch manager will hit the ceiling if he sees the letter, so he files it away in his top drawer, with every intention of showing it to his supervisor after the end of the quarter.

Paperwork is not Ryan's strong suit. He is an action-oriented guy who likes to make things happen and strike while the iron is hot. Yesterday, a woman came into his office after being referred by one of Ryan's wealthier clients. The woman indicated that she lives just a few blocks from the other client, who lives in an exclusive part of town. The woman was wearing expensive jewelry and a fine, mink coat, so when she asked for Ryan's recommendations, Ryan suggested that she buy municipal bonds. The client agreed that munibonds sounded like a good investment. She was too busy to fill out the new account form, so Ryan simply filled it out for her. After all, she is a friend of a wealthy client and lives in an affluent area. Not to mention the expensive jewelry and mink coat. He estimated her net worth to be about $2 million and also estimated her annual income to be upwards of $200,000.

What, if anything, has Ryan done wrong?

4. DENISE DENKO

Denise Denko's investment advisory business has grown substantially over the years. She is no longer a sole proprietor but has taken on several partners and formed a limited partnership.

The advisory partnership has decided to begin taking custody of client funds and securities. There is a rule in the state of Illinois against taking custody, so Denise astutely places the assets in the state of Indiana, in a bank just 35 minutes from her office in South Holland, IL. On her frequent trips across the border into Indiana Denise has developed relationships with several high net worth clients who are residents of Indiana. Last year Denise had only 7 such clients and, therefore, has not registered as an adviser in the state of Indiana.

Last week Denise's firm took on three new partners who together represent a minority interest. Since they are only minority partners, Denise sees no reason to inform the clients, who express little interest in such mundane business matters. In fact, as her clients have complained repeatedly about receiving too much mail from the firm, Denise has decided to send statements of funds and securities held in custody semi-annually to her clients.

What, if anything, has Denise done wrong?

5. Maria Sanchez

Maria Sanchez is a registered representative for XLZ Broker-Dealers in Houston, Texas. Last week Maria solicited several offers for unregistered, exempt securities. Because she was in a hurry to close the sales, she omitted several immaterial facts about the securities.

Maria was in such a hurry one afternoon that she unwittingly took an unsolicited order for an unregistered, non-exempt security.

To increase her sales efforts, Maria decided to tell other agents at the firm that if they would refer clients to her, she would split commissions with them. On Monday, she gave one of her fellow agents a check for $300 based on a referral.

Rushing around Tuesday afternoon, Maria took a phone call from the husband of a discretionary client. The husband said his wife wanted Maria to buy shares of IBM today. The wife was out of town, but since the stock met the client's objectives, Maria purchased 400 shares of IBM.

What, if anything, has Maria done wrong?

6. RYAN REYNOLDS

Ryan Reynolds has finally started to build up his book of business. He was fortunate enough to land a major account with Luis Orlando, a famous shortstop with the Cincinnati Reds. Knowing Mr. Orlando's credibility and fame throughout the state of Ohio, Ryan recently figured out that the best way to land new clients is to show prospects all the excellent investments he has recommended to Mr. Orlando and the appreciation of his assets.

Ryan's firm has expanded their investment banking division substantially. Befriending the director of that department, Ryan has picked up several good tips about companies soon to be acquired by larger firms and has skillfully put his clients into the stocks before the acquisitions have been announced to the public.

Ryan has decided to expand his efforts at the firm. During his lunch hour last week Ryan called some of his best clients to interest them in investing in his brother-in-law's sporting goods store, with three locations in the greater Sandusky metropolitan area. Since the investments were consistent with his clients' objectives, he decided not to bother the branch manager by informing him of the sales. One of Ryan's more successful strategies recently has been to take large orders from Luis Orlando, shortstop for the Cincinnati Reds, in certain thinly traded OTC Bulletin Board stocks. Knowing that orders in excess of 10,000 shares in such stocks usually send the price upwards, Ryan has begun to astutely buy shares for himself and the firm's proprietary account just before placing Mr. Orlando's orders.

What, if anything, is Ryan doing wrong?

7. MARCY MATHERS

The telephone rings, and Marcy Mathers grabs it on the second ring.

"Hello?" she says.

"Marcy? This is Dale Dawson. What have you got for me today?"

Marcy covers the mouthpiece and quietly shuts her office door.

"Well," she says, "you didn't hear this from me, but I just heard that GE is about to buy that little electronics firm we were talking about last week."

"Really? Have they announced anything yet?"

"Nope."

"How do you know then?"

Marcy glances over her shoulder and says, "Let's just say I have it on good authority."

"Oh, okay. How's the electronics company doing without the acquisition?"

"Pretty good. I hear they're about to graduate to the level of being NYSE-listed."

"Wow—their earnings are that good, huh?"

"Yep."

"Hmm, so even if they don't get acquired, their earnings are good enough to be listed, huh?"

"That's exactly right."

What, if anything, has Marcy done wrong?

8. LUCINDA LUBOWSKI

Heather Adams is having lunch today with her friend, Lucinda Lubowski, a new registered representative with M&N Broker-Dealers. Heather doesn't work in the securities industry and doesn't really understand everything Lucinda tells her about her job at M &N. But she finds her friend's job fascinating.

Lucinda is more than a little upset this afternoon, as she explains.

"First," she says, "my supervisor comes up to my desk and says one of my customers is chewing him out. The lady is always sending me angry emails and letters about stuff that isn't even my fault half the time."

"What did your supervisor say when you showed him the angry messages?" Heather asks.

Lucinda pauses to sip her bottled water and snap a bread stick.

"Well," she says, looking at the bread stick, "today was the first day he saw them. I didn't want to bother him with a bunch of angry rants from some woman who thinks the S & P 500 is a NASCAR event."

Heather nods and says, "Oh."

"Anyway," Lucinda says, "eventually the client cools down. They're assigning her account to another rep, and I'll be done with it. Of course, I made a few trades right after, to make up for all the lost commissions."

"Wow. What did the customer say about that?"

Lucinda smiles and says, "She'll never notice."

"How come?" Heather scoots closer to the table and rests her elbows on the burgundy tablecloth.

Lucinda glances over both her shoulders, then leans toward her friend.

"Because I did it off the books."

"How?"

"I deleted the trade confirmation. Monthly statements don't go out for another three and a half weeks. I just increased a couple positions—that lady will never notice an extra 30 shares here and there. She already owns a bunch of Wal-Mart and Home Depot. I just added to her position."

"Wow, that sounds a little too 'Boiler Room', doesn't it?"

"Boiler room," Lucinda says, with a girlish grin. "Isn't Ben Affleck a stud? He can boil my room any time, that's for sure."

Heather playfully smacks her friend's wrist.

"So what else?" she asks, stabbing at her spinach salad with a chilled fork.

"Oh yeah," Lucinda says, "some other customer is all upset because I forgot to tell her that one of the funds I sold her has a high expense ratio."

"What's that?"

Lucinda shrugs and says, "I don't know. I just know it pays the best commissions. All funds have expenses; that's life. Anyway, what I said was accurate. I said it was a no-load fund, which it is. It has a 12 b-1 fee, but all of 'em have 12 b-1 fees."

"What the heck is a 12 b-1 fee?"

"Covers expenses like mailing, advertising and selling the fund."

"Hmm. What does a load cover?"

"Same thing, but it's still a 12 b-1 fee, not a sales load, so I can still call it a no-load fund if I want."

Lucinda takes a bite of chicken salad and chews silently a while.

"I don't have time to hold their hand, you know? I'm trying to meet my sales goals for the quarter. They can read a prospectus."

"More than I can say for myself."

"What?" Lucinda says, sharply. "You think I should have told her it was all laid out in the prospectus?"

Heather wrinkles her forehead. "Oh," she says. "I figured you did."

"Anyway," Lucinda says, "it doesn't matter. I'm gonna make a huge pop on a stock I've been buying for my own account, anyway."

"Really? How do you know for sure?"

"Easy. The company is trading for 15 cents a share now, but they're going to be bought by Microsoft in a couple weeks. Me and another friend have about 3,000 shares each. Just after they announce the deal, me and my friend are going to put in orders to buy 1,000 shares at the same time, every 20 minutes. That should help it along big time."

"Wow. How do you know Microsoft's gonna buy 'em?"

"I used to work at Great Plains, remember? I get juicy details on all kinds of software companies—remember how much I made on my stock when they bought Great Plains?"

"Yeah, I think you might have mentioned it a couple times," Heather says, rolling her eyes in case her friend had missed the sarcasm. "Sounds like you're doing okay on the new job, huh? Except for a few complaints."

"Yeah," Lucinda says. "not too bad. You're still picking up the tab, though. I don't get a commission check for three more weeks."

What, if anything, has Lucinda done wrong?

EXPLANATIONS

There is more than one way to explain the violations you uncovered in the examples. The following should, however, look similar to what you've written yourself. If not, feel free to email or call.

1. Ryan Reynolds

Going "partners on a trade"

WHY: a registered representative may not go "halvsies" with a customer. It's the customer's trade—your recommendation. Only way to share with a customer is to have an approved joint account and only share in proportion to the rep's investment

You can't lose on this stock

WHY: regulators just HATE the phrase "can't lose," because, in fact, the customer CAN lose. If it's a security, there is money at risk. Even on a T-bond, rates could go up and push down the market price of the security

Passing around rumors/inside information

WHY: whatever Ryan is implying to the customer, it's wrong. If it's a rumor, it's prohibited. And if it's true, it's inside information. Either way, don't use rumors or inside information if you want to keep your license and keep yourself out of jail.

Misstatements of material facts

WHY: that little dance Ryan did about "earnings" is fraudulent. If a company is losing money, they're certainly not "earning" squat. Earnings are material to any investor, and especially important to this one.

Churning

WHY: pressuring customers into buying more stock than they feel they can afford is a violation. Both excessive size and excessive frequency of trading are considered churning.

Telling customers a stock is listed when you have no freaking idea

WHY: surprising that this has to be specifically stipulated, as if a rep might think it's okay to BS a customer about a major fact like NYSE listing. But never tell someone a stock is listed, if you really have no clue. Especially in this case where the customer says he doesn't buy penny stocks. If this $3 stock is unlisted then it is, most certainly, a penny stock.

2. Denise Denko

An "investment adviser" is a firm, and an individual can register the firm as a sole proprietorship. No different from a guy who owns a pretzel cart. He's the guy who owns the business, but the business is also registered as an entity with the county/

city/state. The business entity is subject to sales and income tax; it has a bank account in its name; and if he sells the business, he gets to keep his individual self, even after he transfers the assets of the business to the new owner, right?

So, what did Denise do wrong?

Verbal contracts

WHY: all advisory contracts must be in writing and must clearly state the terms of the contract, how the advisor gets paid, whether he/she/they have discretion or custody, etc.

Performance-based compensation

WHY: as a general rule, the adviser may not be paid for performance or through a share of capital gains/appreciation. Only in unique circumstances is that type of contract allowed.

The dreaded A-word

WHY: never tell anyone that securities or a firm or an individual has been "approved" by the Administrator. Regulators don't "approve." If you're real lucky, they *allow*. Just like they'll DIS-allow if you use the dreaded A-word.

Conflicts of interest

WHY: Denise benefits by placing trades through a particular broker-dealer. Her clients might be paying higher commissions, though. That's a conflict of interest that has to be disclosed tot he clients paying the higher commissions, right?

3. Ryan Reynolds

Failure to bring to attention of employer customer complaints

WHY: most reps would probably rather take customer complaints to the shredder rather than to the supervisor, but if they do, they're career could end up in the shredder

Making recommendations without sufficient grounds

WHY: chances are Ryan is right about the financial status of the woman in the mink coat and fine jewelry. But that's not the way to determine suitability. The woman could have borrowed the mink coat and fine jewelry just to make a big impression on Ryan with hopes that he'll give her account extra attention. He needs her to provide financial information, and the idea that he is just filling it in for her based on estimates is a really bad idea. There is no assurance that the information is even close to accurate. How does he even know she has an annual income? Even affluent areas have a few not-so-impressive houses. Or, this customer could be working as an on-site domestic helper, staying in some rich person's coach house and borrowing her employer's wardrobe for the afternoon.

4. DENISE DENKO

Custody of client funds

WHY: Denise's advisory firm operates in Illinois. There is a rule against custody in Illinois (in this test question), so Denise firm can't just hide the money in a neighboring state.

Registration of advisory firms

WHY: if Denise has more than 5 non-institutional clients in Indiana, she has to register as an advisory firm in Indiana

Notify clients of change in partnership

WHY: when the membership changes, clients must be informed promptly, regardless of minority/majority interest

Statement of funds under custody

WHY: Denise shouldn't have custody to begin with, but even if that were okay, she needs to send statements to customers quarterly, not every six months.

5. MARIA SANCHEZ

Believe it or not, Maria Sanchez has done absolutely nothing wrong. If a security is "exempt," it does not have to be registered, so calling something an "unregistered exempt" security is redundant and lots of fun for a writer of Series 63 questions.

If the transaction is exempt, it's okay that the security is unregistered, so, again, she did nothing wrong.

Registered representatives of the same firm can split commissions.

If Maria has discretion, she doesn't even need the husband—or the client—to call her before buying a security that appears to be suitable. That's what having "discretion" over an account means. The customer lets the rep not just make recommendations but actually buy or sell when they think it's time to buy or sell something.

6. RYAN REYNOLDS

This guy Ryan probably ain't gonna last too long in the securities business.

Disclosing identity, affairs of client without permission or court order

WHY: pretty self-explanatory, really. The client probably wouldn't appreciate your telling everybody his business, and neither would the Administrator

Trading on material inside information

WHY: this is exactly what regulators worry about. Many big firms have investment banking divisions, which know ahead of time about big mergers and acquisitions. There is supposed to be a "Chinese Wall" around this division, separating investment banking's hot deals and the registered reps who, naturally, want to give their clients an edge. Ryan has knocked down the wall with a battering ram.

Selling away, private securities transactions

WHY: Ryan has to give his firm notice and get their permission before selling any investments at the firm. He's not pitching a listed or even a publicly traded security. What he's doing is called "selling away," a big no-no. To offer an investment opportunity in his brother-in-law's business, he must get his employer's permission and provide any disclosure documents the firm requires. Or, he could just save his time, because the firm isn't going to let him do it, anyway. Why should they?

Frontrunning

It's a great strategy because it gives Ryan a big advantage, just like if Luis Orlando started corking his bat or taking steroids. However, all three actions are prohibited. Securities professionals may NOT take a position just prior to a large order in order to benefit from the transaction about to take place.

Yes, they take all the fun out of the business these regulators.

7. Marcy Mathers

Marcy must be a good friend of Ryan Reynolds.

Trading on rumors, inside information

WHY: we're not sure if Marcy is spreading rumors or using inside information, but we're sure that either way it's a prohibited activity

Misleading information

WHY: "graduated to the level of NYSE listing" is a misleading statement. Stocks are listed if they have enough shares outstanding and enough national interest. It doesn't mean they're all wonderful investments. They don't even have to have earnings to be listed, so Marcy was very misleading about that point, too.

8. Lucinda Lubowski

Wow, and you thought Ryan and Marcy were ethically impaired, huh? Lucinda is a compliance officer's nightmare and an aggressive regulator's dream come true.

Customer written complaints

WHY: concealing customer written complaints from your supervisor can get you into more trouble than the complaints themselves.

Effecting trades not recorded on the firm's books

WHY: three violations for the price of one. Lucinda clearly churned the account by making trades for the sole purpose of getting commissions, but she also effected a trade not recorded on her firm's books. This is extremely deceitful, no? Buying stocks for your customer's account and trying to hide the fact from the customer and the firm?

Wow.

Regulators like records of all trades, even the ones you don't want anyone to know about.

Especially the ones you don't want anyone to know about.

Concealing information in order to make a profit should qualify as an act of fraud, too, so Lucinda really goofed on that one.

Unethical practices in the sale of investment company shares

WHY: customers don't always understand the confusing terms "sales load," "no load," or "12 b-1 fee," so you have to explain the terms carefully. Lucinda is very cavalier about this, but the regulators expect her to help her clients understand what they're paying for with these loads and/or 12 b-1 fees. She should have at least pointed out that it's explained in the prospectus, no matter how busy she claims to be.

Inside information, market manipulation

WHY: if she really knows Microsoft is going to buy the smaller company, she's trading on inside information. And if she and her friend decide to trade in a way that creates the appearance of excessive interest in the stock, they're engaged in market manipulation.

PRACTICE FINALS

I do not recommend that you do what many students often try, unsuccessfully, when preparing for the Series 63. Many students, unfortunately, buy a batch of practice questions on CD-ROM and practice those questions again and again until they can get a very high score on the disc.

Well, the questions you actually see on the exam will only be *like* the practice questions you do, no matter which practice questions you do. So, the danger is that many students quickly memorize the answers to practice questions, only to be shocked at the testing center where the questions seem to be coming from some other license exam.

You can't memorize test questions for the Series 63. The Series 63 makes you think. You have to understand the concepts and think on your feet. Memorizing the answers to 400 practice questions would only help you if you saw 65 of those questions on the exam—you won't.

But you have to do practice questions in order to get in shape for the test. I've arranged the three practice finals in order of difficulty, starting with the easiest one. Read the explanations carefully and try to imagine other questions that could be written that would cover the same topics.

The website, www.passthe63.com, also has practice questions available. Please make sure that you're not memorizing answers. What you need to do in order to get fit to sit for the Series 63 is develop a good understanding of the concepts, so that you can work with them on exam day.

Ready? See if you can't knock this first exam right out of the ballpark!

PRACTICE FINAL 1

1. **Which of the following is not a person?**
   A. joint stock company
   B. issuer
   C. broker-dealer
   D. 11-year-old child

2. **Anna Ramirez worked for Jefferson Broker-Dealers for three years. If she terminates her employment to take a new job with Brooks Broker-Dealers, who must notify the Administrator?**
   A. Jefferson Broker-Dealers
   B. Anna Ramirez
   C. Brooks Broker-Dealers
   D. all of the above

3. **The Administrator may issue all of the following orders except**
   A. stop
   B. cease and desist
   C. injunction
   D. denial

4. **All the following activities are prohibited except**
   A. sharing commissions with other agents at the firm
   B. pegging
   C. capping
   D. indicating that the Administrator has approved a security

5. **All of the following are prohibited activities except**
   A. capping
   B. arbitrage
   C. selling away
   D. front running

6. **As an investment adviser representative, you know that your clients are easily confused by excessive detail in the statements your firm sends to them. Your firm charges a wrap fee for the accounts that you manage. To avoid confusing your clients, you refer to the fee as a "commission". What is true of this practice?**
   A. it is unethical and prohibited
   B. it is not unethical if prior principal approval has been obtained
   C. it is unethical but not prohibited
   D. wrap fees are illegal post-2002

7. **All of the following are exempt from state-level registration except**
   A. building & loan securities
   B. whiskey warehouse receipts
   C. Microsoft® common stock
   D. T-bonds

8. **All of the following facts must be disclosed to advisory clients except**
   A. precarious financial condition of the advisory firm
   B. legal or regulatory actions against the firm material to evaluation of the firm's integrity
   C. whether the account is discretionary/non-discretionary
   D. whether the Administrator permits custody

9. **Which of the following is defined as a "person"?**
   A. Cincinnati, Ohio
   B. minor
   C. deceased individual
   D. individual declared mentally incompetent by a court of law

10. **Which of the following would most likely be defined as securities?**
    I. futures contract
    II. certificate of 10% ownership in one racehorse
    III. whiskey warehouse receipt
    IV. whole life insurance policy
    A. I, II, III, IV
    B. II, III
    C. II, III, IV
    D. I, II

11. **What do we call the person responsible for administering the USA in a state?**
    A. Governor
    B. Lt. Governor
    C. Your honor
    D. Administrator

12. **The USA grants powers to the Administrator of all the following states except**
    A. state where the offer to sell/offer to buy originated
    B. state where payment for securities was made
    C. state where the offer to sell/offer to buy was directed
    D. state where the offer to sell/offer to buy was accepted

13. **In which of the following cases has a security been offered for sale?**
    A. an investment representative fails to sell a fixed annuity
    B. an investment representative fails to sell a variable annuity
    C. an investment representative donates securities to a non-profit, tax-exempt foundation
    D. an investment represent pledges T-bonds as collateral for a personal loan

14. **In which of the following cases has a security been offered and sold?**
    A. a person makes a gift of assessable stock
    B. a person makes a gift of non-assessable stock
    C. an investment representative fails to sell a fixed annuity
    D. an investment representative fails to sell a variable annuity

15. **The Administrator has the authority under the USA to do all of the following except**
    A. issue stop orders
    B. issue denial orders
    C. issue cease and desist orders in anticipation of a violation
    D. issue injunctions

16. **Which of the following business practices are prohibited?**
    I. recommending transactions based on material, inside information
    II. disclosing the identity and securities holdings of a client in the absence of a court order
    III. deliberately failing to follow a customer's explicit instructions to sell a security
    IV. frontrunning
    A. I, II, IV only
    B. I, II, III, IV
    C. I only
    D. IV only

17. **As an agent for Andersen Broker-Dealers, you are experiencing a very slow month. To keep yourself occupied and pay the bills, you decide to contact your call list of current customers in order to raise enough capital for you and your sister to launch a children's clothing store. The investment meets all of the contacted customers' investment objectives. If you do not inform your employer, this activity**
    A. is fraudulent
    B. is fraudulent and punishable up to 7 years in federal prison
    C. prohibited because children's clothing stores are inherently poor investments
    D. prohibited because you gave your employer no opportunity to supervise your actions

18. **One of your customers is extremely persistent and perturbed. After sending several hostile letters to complain of your handling of the account, the customer refuses to return your next several phone calls. When you receive another angry letter, you decide to discard the letter as well as the others you have received. This practice**
    A. is fraudulent
    B. is prohibited because all written customer complaints must be forwarded to the SEC within 5 business days
    C. is prohibited because all written customer complaints must be forwarded to the Administrator within 5 business days
    D. is prohibited because all written customer complaints must be brought to the attention of your employer

19. **In which case may a registered representative split commissions with her secretary?**
    A. if the principal approves it
    B. if the secretary is registered as an agent
    C. if the split is at least 75/25
    D. never

20. **Recommendations to customers must not be based on which of the following?**
    A. rumors
    B. material inside information
    C. inaccurate material information
    D. all of the above

21. **Your customer's investment objective is steady income without taking on significant default risk. As the registered representative you have discretion over the account. If you purchase penny stocks in companies without positive earnings, this is known as**
    A. an unauthorized trade
    B. misuse of material inside information
    C. churning
    D. fraud

22. **What is true of material facts?**
    A. the agent must choose which material facts to include and exclude from presentations to clients
    B. they must not be disseminated or acted upon
    C. omitting or misstating them is unlawful and fraudulent
    D. they need not be disclosed to large, institutional clients

23. **A client's investment risk would be reduced by all of the following aspects of a security except**
    A. payment of principal and interest is guaranteed by the U.S. Treasury
    B. payment of principal and interest is guaranteed by a large state with adequate financial resources
    C. the stock is listed on the NYSE
    D. the bond's credit rating has been raised to AAA

24. **All of the following business practices are prohibited except**
    A. failing to state all facts about a security
    B. commingling
    C. failing to state all material facts about a security
    D. failing to obtain customer financial information prior to providing recommendations

25. **What is a private investment company?**
    A. an open-end fund investing exclusively in private companies
    B. a closed-end fund investing primarily in private companies
    C. a private company that provides financing for business ventures, i.e. a venture capital firm
    D. an open-end fund that does not disclose its holdings more than biennially

26. **In order to register as a broker-dealer in the state, the firm must do all of the following except**
    A. file a consent to service of process
    B. pay required fees
    C. register all principals at the firm
    D. have at least three principals with MBA degrees or their doctoral equivalent

27. **As long as the advice is not an integral component of the practice, all of the following professionals will most likely qualify for an exemption to state registration except**
    A. lawyer
    B. teacher
    C. accountant
    D. economist

28. **Which of the following persons are investment adviser representatives?**
    I.   individual hired to answer telephones, emails, and faxes for an investment adviser
    II.   individual hired to solicit services of the advisory firm
    III. individual supervising those who solicit the services of the advisory firm
    IV.   an investment adviser with 11 non-institutional clients
    A.   I, II, III only
    B.   II, III only
    C.   I, II, III, IV
    D.   III only

29. **What is true of a broker-dealer registering a successor firm?**
    A.   a fee is required with the filing
    B.   the successor firm must be in existence at the time of filing
    C.   the registration is valid for the unexpired portion of the broker-dealer's registration
    D.   the successor firm must have the same name and structure as the broker-dealer

30. **What is a fiduciary?**
    A.   the judge presiding over an applicant's appeal of a denial order
    B.   the president of a financial institution
    C.   a person charged with managing investments for another person
    D.   an agent for a non-discretionary customer

31. **An out-of-state investment adviser is excluded from the definition of "investment adviser" in the state if**
    A.   the firm had no more than 5 clients the past 12 months
    B.   the firm had no more than 10 clients the past 12 months
    C.   the firm had no more than 25 clients the past 12 months
    D.   the firm has more than $5 million of assets under management

32. **Which of the following is a security?**
    A.   whole life policy
    B.   term life policy
    C.   fixed annuity
    D.   variable life policy

33. **All of the following securities are exempt except**
    A.   T-bonds
    B.   ADR's
    C.   T-bills
    D.   GNMA

34. **Which TWO of the following statements are true concerning methods of securities registration at the state level?**
    I.   registration by coordination becomes effective 10 days after the SEC effective or "release" date
    II.   registration by coordination becomes effective at the state level concurrently with the federal effectiveness, provided the Administrator has not entered an order to deny
    III. the cooling off period for the SEC is a minimum of 20 days
    IV.   the cooling off period for the SEC is a maximum of 20 days
    A.   I, III
    B.   I, IV
    C.   II, III
    D.   II, IV

35. **All of the following securities are exempt from state-level registration and advertising filing requirements except**
    A.   bonds issued by the City of Montreal
    B.   bonds issued by the government of Quebec
    C.   bonds issued by the government of Canada
    D.   bonds issued by a Canadian corporation

36. **Which of the following are exempt transactions?**
    A.   isolated non-issuer transactions effected through a registered broker-dealer
    B.   transactions between an issuer and its underwriters
    C.   transactions between an issuer and a financial institution
    D.   all of the above

37. **If the issuer and underwriters have filed a registration by qualification statement with the Administrator, before the securities have been cleared for sale they may distribute**
    A.   a tombstone
    B.   a preliminary prospectus
    C.   the registration statement
    D.   all of the above

38. **No specific response from the Administrator is required for securities filed under which of the following methods?**
    I.   qualification
    II.   filing
    III.   coordination
    IV.   notice filing
    A.   I only
    B.   I, II and III only
    C.   II only
    D.   II, III, and IV only

39. **The state registration statement for a security registered by coordination must include all of the following except**
    A.   any agreement with or among the underwriters
    B.   amount offered in all states
    C.   all states in which the security will be offered
    D.   a stop order from another state affecting the offering in that state

40. **Which of the following are exempt securities?**
    A.   building and loan securities
    B.   bank securities
    C.   bonds issued by a company with common stock listed on the NYSE
    D.   all of the above

41. **All of the following are exempt transactions except**
    A.   initial public offering
    B.   a sheriff liquidates assets seized from a convicted felon
    C.   a Marshall liquidates assets seized from a convicted felon
    D.   transaction between an issuer and its underwriters

42. **A private placement is an exempt transaction under the USA that allows an issuer to solicit a maximum of how many investors in a 12-month period?**
    A.   35
    B.   10
    C.   100
    D.   1,000

43. **Which of the following are not securities as defined under the USA?**
    A.   whiskey warehouse receipts
    B.   bank securities
    C.   interests in multilevel distributorships
    D.   fixed annuities

44. **If a registrant can not be located, the Administrator would likely issue a**
    A.   stop order
    B.   suspension
    C.   cancellation
    D.   denial

45. **Which TWO of the following orders may the Administrator issue even without prior notice and opportunity for hearing?**
    I.   cease and desist
    II.   summary suspension of a pending registration
    III. stop order
    IV.   denial order
    A.   I, II
    B.   I, III
    C.   II, III
    D.   II, IV

46. **Which of the following powers does the USA grant to the Administrator?**
    A.   power to investigate in and outside the state
    B.   power to publish violations
    C.   power to allow items to be omitted from registration statements
    D.   all of the above

47. **An agent's application for state registration may be denied if it is in the public interest and the agent**
    A.   claims to have earned an MBA from a prestigious school when, in fact, she has yet to complete her undergraduate work
    B.   has been subject to adjudication during the past 10 years under federal securities law
    C.   has been convicted of a non-securities related felony 7 years ago
    D.   all of the above

48. **Which of the following statements are true concerning federal covered advisers?**
    A.   if the firm manages over $25 million, they are federal covered
    B.   federal covered advisers are subject to the Administrator's powers to enforce antifraud regulations
    C.   federal covered advisers must file a consent to service of process
    D.   all of the above

49. **The penalties for violating the securities laws of a state include**
    A. administrative proceedings
    B. criminal penalties
    C. civil liability
    D. all of the above

50. **The major effect of NSMIA is that it**
    A. granted more power to state securities Administrators
    B. allowed states to require more stringent filing standards and financial requirements than that required at the federal level
    C. eliminated the need for dual registration for most securities
    D. all of the above

51. **All of the following are federal covered securities except**
    A. GNMA
    B. T-bills
    C. Chicago revenue bonds
    D. OTC Bulletin Board stock

52. **Brian Bonyers is a beginning broker at Baker-Brooks Broker-Dealership. Recently, Brian signed up a new customer who was too busy to complete the suitability section of the new account form. The customer did, however, specify a home address within a very affluent section of a Bryant County suburb. Knowing both the mean and median home values of that exclusive area, Brian decides to recommend municipal securities and other tax-exempt investments to the client. What is true of this case?**
    A. this is a standard procedure
    B. this is a prohibited practice that violates suitability requirements
    C. this is fraudulent, punishable up to 7 years in a state penitentiary
    D. this an example of misuse of material inside information

53. **All of the following are prohibited practices except**
    A. effecting transactions not recorded on the books of the broker-dealership
    B. soliciting orders for unregistered exempt securities
    C. telling a customer that this is a can't-lose investment
    D. soliciting orders for unregistered non-exempt securities

54. **In order for an investment adviser to act as a principal for its own account in the purchase or sale of a security with a client, which of the following must take place?**
    A. disclose potential conflict of interest to the client in writing
    B. obtain client's written consent
    C. both
    D. neither

55. An investment adviser representative is attempting to land a new client who displays an inordinate fascination with technical analysis. The adviser representative has experienced tremendous success with his stock selections over the past several years through careful, painstaking fundamental analysis. But, since the customer prefers technical analysis, the adviser representative indicates that he does, in fact, often use the "technicals" of a certain company before selecting a stock, by which he means the fundamentals of the company, i.e. EPS, P/E ratio, capitalization ratios, etc. "So, you're a technical analyst, then?" the client asks. "I sure am, sir," the investment adviser responds." What is true of this case?
    A. it is perfectly acceptable as long as the adviser representative meant what he said in earnest and *ipso facto tremeris* no longer applies
    B. it is a prohibited practice and may constitute a deceit or fraud upon the client
    C. it is not prohibited if the sales pitch receives prior principal approval
    D. it is prohibited unless accompanied by a prospectus

56. A highly regarded Wall Street Analyst buys large blocks of thinly traded issues a few days before issuing positive reports on those companies. What is true of this case?
    A. if he does not disclose his ownership position in the securities he is covering, he could be suspected of market manipulation
    B. even if he provides disclosure of his ownership position this always constitutes a fraud
    C. this would only be fraudulent for municipal securities
    D. this is a perfectly acceptable Wall Street practice and no disclosure is necessary

57. An investment advisory firm is established as a partnership. If the partnership admits three new members having a minority interest
    A. assignment of contract has occurred
    B. this event need not be disclosed to clients
    C. this event must be disclosed to clients promptly
    D. this is a fraudulent, unethical business practice

58. The definition of "investment contract" as a result of the Howey Decision is that the instrument in question displays which of the following characteristics?
    A. represents an interest in a common enterprise
    B. money is at risk
    C. owner hopes to benefit through the efforts of others
    D. all of the above

59. As a registered representative for XL Broker-Dealers, you will, of course, be paid commissions on every customer buy and sell order. Therefore you should
    A. encourage customers to buy and sell frequently
    B. encourage customers to sell frequently
    C. encourage all customers to buy large blocks of securities
    D. consider suitability before recommending any transaction

60. All of the following are securities except
    A. assessable stock
    B. non-assessable stock
    C. note
    D. commodity futures contract

ANSWERS PRACTICE FINAL 1

1. ANSWER: D

EXPLANATION: "person" does not necessarily mean "human being." A human being is a "natural person," but that's just one little *example* of a "person." A person could be a company, a government—basically ANYTHING not dead, a minor, or mentally incompetent as declared by a court of law.

2. ANSWER: D

EXPLANATION: lifted directly from the USA. The firms and the rep must all notify the Administrator. If you ever got a funky question about an investment adviser representative leaving one federal covered adviser to work for another, then I would tell the test only the adviser rep would notify, since the firms are subject to SEC jurisdiction.

I would also hope you don't get a stupid question like that on the test.

But you might.

3. ANSWER: C

EXPLANATION: only a court can issue an injunction. Just as only a court can sentence a violator to prison.

I bet the Administrator might have some influence over either outcome, but they only have the power to issue the following: cease & desist, denial, suspension, revocation, and stop orders. All of those except "cease & desist" must first give the party notice and an opportunity for a hearing, where the Administrator has to, like, prove his case. And, if you don't like his decision to deny, suspend, or revoke your license, you get to appeal the decision in court. You must file that appeal in 60 days.

4. ANSWER: A

EXPLANATION: as long as the other agent is registered and works either for your firm or a related entity (subsidiary, for example), it's okay to share commissions. Pegging and capping are forms of market manipulation where we try to set a price for a stock in the secondary market. Pegging = pushing a stock up. Capping = keeping a stock down.

Don't do that if you can help it.

And don't use the dreaded A-word when talking about the big A. The Big A doesn't Approve or Disapprove. Neither does the SEC.

5. ANSWER: B

EXPLANATION: arbitrage is an enjoyable activity whereby you buy IBM on the NYSE at $85 while you *simultaneously* sell IBM for $85.25 on one of the regional exchanges in Chicago, Philadelphia, Boston, etc. That's known technically as "arbitrage" or a "real good day."

Capping is market manipulation. Selling away could also be referred to as a "private securities transaction." A registered rep can not offer investments in anything his/her firm doesn't know about and doesn't sponsor. Like trying to find investors who will pony up $50,000 each to help your sister start a bed and breakfast. Might be a good investment, but it isn't a listed or NASDAQ stock; in fact, it don't even sound like stock at all. You'd have to get permission and provide disclosure to your firm if you wanted to do something like that. Front running is also a very enjoyable activity whereby you take an order for a customer to buy 20,000 shares of some thinly traded penny stock. Since you know that buy order will probably push up the price of the stock, you buy some for yourself or the firm and THEN put in the customer's big order.

Hmm. Sound too good to be true?

It is.

It's called frontrunning.

Don't do that.

6. ANSWER: A

EXPLANATION: it ain't true, so it's definitely unethical and prohibited. A "wrap fee" includes a fee for investment advice/money management. A commission is just a little juice you gotta pay to buy or sell a stock. Be real clear on the difference with your customers. Don't fall for an answer that says it's okay if the principal says so. Not.

7. ANSWER: B

EXPLANATION: whiskey warehouse receipts are securities and they have no exemption from registration. T-bonds are exempt at the federal and therefore the state level—that's the effect of NSMIA. If the feds say you're cool, the states have to be cool with you, too. Microsoft is a NASDAQ NMS stock, so it's covered SPECIFICALLY by the SEC/feds. Building & Loan (or basically anything related to banking) securities get an exemption, too.

Why?

Because they do. Forget logic—these are just the rules.

8. ANSWER: D

EXPLANATION: the contract has to state whether the adviser has discretion, but custody is between the firm and the Administrator. The firm sees if there's a rule against custody. In the absence of a rule against it, the firm takes custody and notifies the Administrator. Disclosing shaky financial situations or regulatory problems might make it tough for the advisory firm to land new clients—tough. Do you want a money manager who, apparently, can't manage their own money or stay out of trouble?

Remember, these rules are out to protect investors from such firms. If no protection is needed, there is no need for a rule or an order. That's why the Administrative orders to deny, suspend, and revoke always state that the order is in the public interest and provides necessary protection to investors.

If not, the heck with it.

But, if the investors need protection and the action provides it, go for it.

Hmm, some of this stuff actually makes sense.

9. ANSWER: A

EXPLANATION: nobody misses this question. Even if you did, take a mulligan and pretend you didn't. Missing this question is like getting into the big game, stepping onto the court, and bouncing the ball right off your foot out of bounds.

Ouch.

Don't do that if you can help it. Make the lay-ups without breaking a sweat.

There will be plenty of other opportunities for sweating.

10. ANSWER: B

EXPLANATION: you'll probably never forget that a whiskey warehouse receipt is a security, even if you'll probably never actually see one. So, if you weren't sure about the 10% ownership interest, you still knew that choice "II" was in your answer, because choice "II" came as a package with choice "III," the whiskey warehouse receipt. Whole life, term life, fixed annuity . . . those are NOT securities. So, with a little test-taking skill, you eliminate choice "IV," which eliminates answers "A" and "C."

And that's how you kick the Series 63's butt every day, twice on Sundays.

11. ANSWER: D

EXPLANATION: You're welcome. Enjoy the few gifts this stingy exam gives you.

12. ANSWER: B

EXPLANATION: doesn't matter where payment was sent. Somebody tries to sell the security from a telephone in Illinois—Illinois is the state where the offer originated. Somebody listens to the offer by phone in Kentucky—Kentucky is where the offer was received/directed into. If that somebody calls back the rep from West Virginia and says she'll take it—West Virginia is the state where the offer was accepted. If the check was dropped off at a mailbox in Pennsylvania, nobody cares. But the Administrators in IL, KY, and WV all have authority.

13. ANSWER: B

EXPLANATION: the rep offered the fixed annuity, too, but that's not a security. Pledging and donating are not offers or sales. Rather, those activities are defined as "pledging" and "donating."

14. ANSWER: A

EXPLANATION: a gift of assessable stock is considered both an offer and a sale, while a gift of NON-assessable stock is not.

What's assessable stock?

Do you really care?

I sure hope not.

But some of you do, so it's stock that can be assessed a fee and, I believe, comes with further purchasing rights.

Anyway, choices C and D were offers, and only one of them (variable annuity) involved a security. So, the worst choice you could have made was C, since it was neither a sale nor a security.

Of course, there's really no need to rub it in.

15. ANSWER: D

EXPLANATION: only a court can issue an injunction. The Administrator can ask the court to issue an injunction, but he has to ask nicely and have a pretty good reason. Notice that the cease and desist can be issued even BEFORE anything wrong has been done. I bet a lot of school principals wish they could tell certain kids to go take a time-out because it looks likely that they will break some of the school's rules by the end of the day. Not a punishment, just an order to stop whatever you were thinking of doing. Cease and desist. We'll get to the bottom of the whole thing after that.

16. ANSWER: B

EXPLANATION: don't they all just kind of sound bad? That's the sense you need to develop for this exam. You need to be able to "sense" prohibited acts, and acts of fraud/deceit. That way, you should be able to use process of elimination to get, like, 90% of the business practices questions right.

Which is a great way to win this struggle called the Series 63.

17. ANSWER: D

EXPLANATION: this is an example of "selling away." If you want to offer some investment opportunity outside the scope of your employment as a registered representative, you have to get the broker-dealer's permission (good luck) and provide any disclosure that they demand.

In other words, don't go there.

There was nothing fraudulent going on, just a real bad idea. That's sort of the difference between fraud and a "prohibited practice." Fraud involves deceiving a client in order to make a profit. Prohibited practices are things you just don't want to do. You didn't deceive any clients; you just screwed up at the firm, and the Administrator ain't too happy about it, neither. If you did something you weren't supposed to do—that's a prohibited act. If you deceived a client in order to sell something, and you knew it was wrong when you did it—what in the heck were you thinking? That's fraud!

Don't do that.

18. ANSWER: D

EXPLANATION: this question is just a bunch of words. If you're willing to read them all, you just have to ask yourself where you forward written complaints—to your supervisor, principal. Not directly to the regulators.

It's not fraud—you didn't deceive anyone while selling securities. You just tried to play Arthur Andersen with a customer's written complaint.

Don't do that—it's prohibited.

19. ANSWER: B

EXPLANATION: gotta be licensed/registered to receive commissions. Remember that if something is wrong, it doesn't become okay just because the principal approves it. In other words, the regulators are holding YOU accountable, too. That's why they're making you take this test—having taken and passed this exam, you'll have no excuse for the bad stuff you do in the future. You get a general sense of what's okay and what isn't from this test, and you learn several specifics, too. That means you've been fairly warned, so your chances of ever proving ignorance of a particular rule are pretty slim. Your principal would get in trouble for saying something prohibited was just fine by him, but you'll get in trouble for doing it, too. You knew better; that's what passing the 63 means to a regulator.

20. ANSWER: D

EXPLANATION: this one's a lay-up. Don't use rumors, false information, or material inside information.

They take all the fun out of this business, indeed.

21. ANSWER: A

EXPLANATION: when you have discretion over a customer's account, you have to buy what's suitable for the customer. If you buy something

UN-suitable, they call that an "unauthorized trade." The customer only authorizes you to buy stuff that makes sense given his investment objectives. They don't authorize you to do whatever the heck you want for whatever reason you decide.

Right?

If you're tempted by the "fraud," choice, remember that fraud is lying, cheating, or deceiving a customer in order to make some money off him. He says he only buys stocks with positive earnings. So you sell him a stock without earnings and just lie that they do, in fact, have all kinds of earnings.

Total fraud. Buying an inappropriate stock is not fraudulent; it's just a real bad idea. A prohibited act, not necessarily fraudulent. Heck, you might have goofed. You really thought it was a great stock for the client—you might just be displaying poor judgment rather than outright fraud.

22. ANSWER: C

EXPLANATION: you don't choose which material facts to disclose and which ones not to—if it's material, you disclose it. Not just to some customers, but all customers.

23. ANSWER: C

EXPLANATION: being listed and being good ain't the same thing. To be listed the stock needs to have a certain number of shares and enough national interest to make it worth the exchange's while. But there are plenty of dogs on the NYSE and NASDAQ. Or maybe you never bought any FMO or JDSU?

24. ANSWER: A

EXPLANATION: what would "all facts about a security" be? The size of the certificates? The type of paper and ink used by the printer?

Only MATERIAL facts need to be disclosed; omit all the unnecessary stuff. If they didn't write the rules that way, some weasel of a customer could try to come after you after losing money on a stock because you forgot to tell him that the average height of the corporation's vice-presidents is 5 feet 9 inches.

Who cares? It was completely IM-material.

Now, if you forgot to mention the lawsuits against the company, or the auditor's doubts about the business remaining as a going concern . . . well, that stuff's material.

25. ANSWER: C

EXPLANATION: choice "C" explains the concept all by itself

26. ANSWER: D

EXPLANATION: we don't necessarily have to have even ONE MBA—the other three are required, though.

27. ANSWER: D

EXPLANATION: the "E" is for "Engineer," not "E-conomist."

28. ANSWER: B

EXPLANATION: anyone selling the services of the firm, providing advice, making recommendations, or supervising folks who do that stuff is defined as an investment adviser representative and must register. The federal covered adviser is NOT an adviser representative, just like a broker-dealer is not an agent. One is the firm—the other just represents the firm. Sammy Sosa plays for the Cubs. Sammy Sosa, however, is NOT the Chicago Cubs. He just plays for them, the way an agent plays for/represents a firm called a broker-dealer and an investment adviser representative represents a firm called an investment adviser.

29. ANSWER: C

EXPLANATION: the four answer choices sort of provide the answer to the question—no fee is required; the firm doesn't have to be in existence yet and does not have to have the same name. Your broker-dealer is a partnership changing to a corporation with a different name. You register the successor firm without paying a fee. The successor firm's registration is good for the unexpired portion of the broker-dealer's registration.

Exciting stuff.

30. ANSWER: C

EXPLANATION: a fiduciary makes investment decisions for other people: trustee, pension fund manager, custodian in an UGMA, registered rep with discretion. They all look out for others and must be faithful (**fid**uciary/ **fid**elity) to the other party(ies).

31. ANSWER: A

EXPLANATION: this is called the "de minimus exemption" which means, in the original Latin, "so few it don't matter." No more than 5 non-institutional buyers. As many institutional buyers as you want, but only 5 little guys. But, if your firm is <u>in</u> the state, you must register. We're only talking about OUT-of-state firms here.

32. ANSWER: D

EXPLANATION: if your money is secure, it's not a security. It's only a security if your money is NOT secure.

Seriously.

The fixed annuity promises a certain payout, as do those insurance policies.

Not the variable annuity. Guess what its payment does?

It varies.

Hmm.

So, since your money isn't secure, now *that's* a security.

Perhaps a break is in order?

33. ANSWER: B

EXPLANATION: ADR's have no specific exemption—Treasuries and agencies are exempt securities that do not have to be registered.

34. ANSWER: C

EXPLANATION: with the SEC, you'll be cooling off a minimum of 20 days, usually much, much longer than just 20 days. At the state level, securities registered by coordination are effective concurrently/ simultaneously with the federal/SEC effectiveness, unless the Administrator has a real problem with the whole thing.

Nothing is effective a particular number of days after federal effectiveness. It's either effective concurrent with federal (Coordination, Filing) or whenever the Administrator says so (Qualification).

35. ANSWER: D

EXPLANATION: Canadian governments, not corporations, are granted exemptions. For Canada, it doesn't matter if the government is national, provincial, or local. In all other cases, though, only the national/federal government securities are exempt, not the provincial/state/local government securities. So Mexico City bonds are non (NOT)-exempt; bonds issued by the federal government of Mexico are exempt. Bonds issued by Paris are non (NOT)-exempt; bonds issued by the government of France are exempt.

And then for Canada it's different—ALL the governments there get an exemption.

But, still, not the corporations.

Bet you're glad you know this, ey?

The test will be glad, too, ey.

36. ANSWER: D

EXPLANATION: stuff to memorize

37. ANSWER: D

EXPLANATION: more stuff to memorize. Why would they circulate the registration statement itself?

Maybe cause they're real cheap? Or cause they know nobody reads whatever they hand 'em, anyway?

38. ANSWER: D

EXPLANATION: only in qualification does the issuer have to wait for the Administrator to give a specific response of "go ahead and sell 'em." The other methods are for issuers dealing with the SEC and just keeping the Administrator informed, too.

39. ANSWER: B

EXPLANATION: the Administrator wants to know which states you're selling in, but he doesn't need the total amount for each state. He needs the total amount for his state. And he really does want to know if anybody else has a problem with your securities. He might even buy 'em lunch just to talk about it a while.

40. ANSWER: D

EXPLANATION: the question explains itself.

41. ANSWER: A

EXPLANATION: IPO's get no exemption . . . unless they're being done by certain companies that qualify for a "blue chip" exemption. The little guys doing IPO's get no exemption, much as they'd like to get one. The other three are definitely exempt transactions, so they don't have to be registered with the Administrator, and it doesn't matter if the securities are registered, either.

42. ANSWER: B

EXPLANATION: if you keep the number of investors to 10, it wouldn't matter if they were institutional or non-institutional buyers. If you go over that number, you have to keep the number of non-institutional buyers to 10, while the number of institutions is basically unlimited.

43. ANSWER: D

EXPLANATION: if it has a fixed, guaranteed payment, it is NOT a security

44. ANSWER: C

EXPLANATION: when the "person" is dead, declared mentally incompetent, no longer in business, or can not be located, the Administrator cancels the registration.

45. ANSWER: A

EXPLANATION: if the registration is pending, he can "summarily suspend" it before giving the person notice and opportunity for a hearing. They'll get their notice and opportunity for a hearing, but that's after the summary suspension is issued. For stop, denial, suspension, and revocation orders, the notice and opportunity for hearing come first. Not for cease & desist and summary suspension orders.

Now it's really getting interesting, huh?

46. ANSWER: D

EXPLANATION: yeah, the Administrator can do just about anything shy of sending you to jail or issuing an injunction. Those actions require a court of law.

47. ANSWER: D

EXPLANATION: those all look like good reasons to me. She's already been in trouble, or she's lying on her registration? I'd say we should deny this one, right?

48. ANSWER: D

EXPLANATION: all true statements. Federal covered advisers are filing their paperwork with the SEC and submitting to SEC inspections. But, if they commit fraud, the state securities Administrator still has the power to enforce anti-fraud rules on their big, federal-covered attitude. They also provide a consent to service of process so that the aggrieved party can serve papers on them by simply serving them on the Administrator, who is always more than willing to accept them on their behalf.

49. ANSWER: D

EXPLANATION: all three, absolutely

50. ANSWER: C

EXPLANATION: NSMIA reduced the state's powers and created a new class of securities called "federal covered" securities, which register with the SEC, rather than sweating it out in each and every state. The issuers might provide a "notice filing" to the state, but their securities aren't subject to the state's "merit test" or requirements to file all advertising and have that get the okay, too. Cuts through the red tape. If you're a small issuer, you'll be stuck jumping through all the regulatory hoops at the state level, but NSMIA says if you're an investment company, a listed stock, a NASDAQ stock, or a variable annuity, you can just register with the SEC/federal, not the states. You provide a notice filing which is exactly what it sounds like—notification. I'm notifying you, sir; I'm NOT asking for your permission.

51. ANSWER: D

EXPLANATION: if it's exempt at the federal level, it's automatically exempt at the state level. So Treasuries, agencies, and revenue bonds are exempt at both levels. OTC stocks must be part of the National Market System, which is NASDAQ and NASDAQ'S Small Cap "list" of stocks, to be federal covered. Bulletin Board/Pink Sheet stocks don't get the blue chip exemption, so they're stuck dealing with the Administrator on the Administrator's turf.

Harsh.

52. ANSWER: B

EXPLANATION: the rep is assuming too much and being lazy. Get the net worth, the income level, the specifics of THIS client. Don't just think of her as "some rich person" and start making recommendations. Even if you thought it was fraudulent, nothing is punishable up to 7 years in a state penitentiary. The maximum penalties at the state level are three years, $5,000 fine or both.

53. ANSWER: B

EXPLANATION: if it's exempt it doesn't need to be registered.

54. ANSWER: C

EXPLANATION: the adviser has to make it clear that the stock is being sold out of inventory to the customer, or purchased from the customer for inventory. See the possible conflict? I'm charging you to make a recommendation, but now I'm either trying to sell you something of mine, or buy something of yours for my collection. Hmm, when I try to buy something, I try to talk the price down; when I sell something, I try to talk the price up, right? Whom does that benefit? The customer? Not really—there's the conflict. So, the adviser must disclose the potential conflict and get the customer's written consent ahead of time. Broker-dealers have to disclose the "principal" capacity of their transactions with customers, but they don't need prior written consent. Just a heads up.

55. ANSWER: B

EXPLANATION: wow, this dude's answer to the client is totally misleading. He's NOT a technical analyst, but he's leading the customer to believe he is in order to close a sale.

Yowza. It's definitely prohibited and smells like fraud/deceit.

Right?

Choice A was bogus. No idea what "ipso facto tremeris" means, let alone when it would or wouldn't apply. And, again, just because the principal says it's okay don't make it okay.

56. ANSWER: A

EXPLANATION: sounds like standard practice during the tech bubble, but that's partly why it bubbled and then popped. Lots of professionals held big positions in stocks, then went on TV talking them up to help pump up the price.

Nice work when you can get it.

Nowadays, they all disclose whether they have a position in the stock they're praising.

57. ANSWER: C

EXPLANATION: when the membership of the partnership changes (death, admission, withdrawal), this must be disclosed to clients promptly. If the members represented a majority, assignment of contract would have occurred.

58. ANSWER: D

EXPLANATION: this way no matter how weird it sounds, a 10% ownership of a racehorse is an investment contract and therefore a security. It represents an investment in a common enterprise—you and all the other owners. You could lose money, and you hope to benefit through the efforts of others: the jockey, the trainer, and—most of all—the horse. So we get to regulate this, too. Whiskey warehouse receipts, even. Oh yeah, we define things carefully so we can regulate everything we want to regulate and NOT bother regulating stuff we want to exclude, like fixed annuities.

59. ANSWER: D

EXPLANATION: if you missed this one, you're not thinking about what these regulatory tests would want to hear. Always tell a regulator what you know they want to hear. Ever attend a parochial school with tough disciplinary policies?

Yes, Ma'am, I sure will remember to bring my homework tomorrow. No, Ma'am, I sure don't find anything particularly amusing about my behavior this morning.

60. ANSWER: D

EXPLANATION: commodities/futures are not securities. Options on them-there commodities/futures ARE securities.

Aren't you glad you signed up for this abuse?

Practice Final 2

1. **All of the following are considered dishonest or unethical practices in the securities business except**
   A. an agent describes an investment company share as being "no-load" even though the fund charges a 12b-1 equal to .25% of average net assets
   B. an agent describes an investment company share as being "no-load" even though the fund charges a 12b-1 greater than .25% of average net assets
   C. an agent selling investment company shares with a front-end load fails to disclose any breakpoints that may be available to reduce sales charges
   D. an agent selling investment company shares with a front-end load fails to disclose any Letter of Intent features that may be available to reduce sales charges

2. **Which of the following are considered dishonest or unethical practices?**
   A. an agent discloses the current yield of a mutual fund without clearly explaining the difference between current yield and total return
   B. an agent states that an investment company's performance is similar to that of a savings account, CD, or other bank deposit account without disclosing that the shares of the investment company are not guaranteed or insured by the FDIC or any other governmental agency
   C. an agent states that a government bond mutual fund portfolio holds securities guaranteed against default by the U.S. Government without also disclosing other risks such as interest rate risk
   D. all of the following

3. **Which of the following are considered dishonest or unethical practices?**
   A. an agent combines capital gains distributions with income distributions to disclose yield of an investment company share to a potential client
   B. an agent provides 1-, 5-, and 10-year projections of mutual fund performance
   C. an agent recommends to a customer several different mutual fund portfolios with similar investment objectives without reasonable grounds to believe that such recommendation is suitable based on the customer's objectives, financial situation, other securities holdings, and any associated transaction charges or other fees
   D. all of the above

4. **What is true of a prospectus for Investment Company shares?**
   A. delivering a prospectus to the prospect satisfies all disclosure requirements of an agent/broker-dealer
   B. no-load mutual fund shares often involve 12b-1 fees
   C. mutual fund prospectuses typically provide projections for 1-, 5-, and 10-year periods
   D. capital gains are commonly combined with income distributions in order to calculate the annual yield of an investment company share

5. **All of the following statements concerning dissemination of information on products and services via the Internet are true except**
   A. information on products/services may be disseminated to residents of states where the firm and/or representative are unregistered
   B. transactions via the Internet are not allowed with residents of states where the firm and/or representative are unregistered
   C. the Interpretative Order concerning Internet communications applies equally to state-registered persons and persons not subject to the Administrator's jurisdiction as a result of NSMIA
   D. the broker-dealer or investment adviser must first authorize the dissemination of information on products/services and retains responsibility for the communications

6. **Which TWO of the following represent true statements?**
   I. Investment advisers are fiduciaries who must act primarily for the benefit of their clients
   II. The Administrator has no power over federal covered advisers engaging in fraudulent, deceptive activities
   III. Federal covered advisers must file a consent to service of process with the Administrator
   IV. An investment adviser does not have to disclose to a client in writing before rendering advice that the adviser will receive a commission for executing the trade resulting from the client's acceptance of the advice
   A. I, III
   B. I, IV
   C. II, IV
   D. II, III

7. **An investment adviser may borrow money and securities from all of the following except**
   A. a broker-dealer
   B. a financial institution engaged in the business of making loans
   C. an affiliate of the adviser
   D. a client

8. **Which of the following statements is true concerning investment advisers with custody of client securities and/or funds?**
   A. this practice is illegal in all cases
   B. the adviser must send to clients monthly an itemized statement showing the funds and securities in the adviser's custody and all debits, credits, and transactions over such period
   C. at least once per year the adviser must schedule an inspection by a CPA or public accountant, who will file a statement with the Administrator promptly afterward
   D. unless the Administrator specifically prohibits custody of client funds/securities, the adviser may take custody of client funds/securities if written notice is sent to the Administrator

9. **Which of the following four statements represent true statements concerning broker-dealers operating on the premises of a bank, savings & loan, or other financial institution?**
   I. wherever practical, the broker-dealer services shall be conducted in a physical location distinct from the area in which the financial institution's retail deposits are taken
   II. in all cases the broker-dealer must clearly distinguish its services from the financial institution's retail deposit-taking activities
   III. in those situations where physical space is limited, the broker-dealer may occupy the same physical space where retail deposits are taken, provided that the broker-dealer takes greater care to distinguish its services from those of the financial institution

IV.   an arrangement whereby a broker-dealer operates on the premises of a financial
       institution taking retail deposits is referred to as a "networking arrangement"
A.   I, II, III, IV
B.   I, II
C.   I, II, III
D.   II, IV

10. **Which of the following persons would be defined as investment advisers under the USA?**
    A.   an advisory firm with no office in the state who has five non-accredited clients residing
          in the state
    B.   an advisory firm with no office in the state who advises for compensation 11 pension
          funds as to the value or advisability of investing in particular securities
    C.   an advisory firm with an office in the state who advises for compensation 11 pension
          funds as to the value or advisability of investing in particular securities
    D.   an advisory firm in the state whose sole clients are Investment Companies as defined
          under the Investment Company Act of 1940

11. **All of the following are persons except**
    A.   joint-stock company
    B.   broker-dealer
    C.   corporation
    D.   7-year-old child

12. **Which of the following persons would be defined as an "agent" under the USA?**
    A.   a broker-dealer with an office in the state whose clients include pension funds, mutual
          funds, and other institutional investors
    B.   an individual representing a non-exempt issuer in an unsolicited transaction
    C.   a broker-dealer selling only non-exempt securities to clients not averse to the risks
          involved
    D.   an individual representing GE in the sale of GE stock to GE employees for which a
          commission is received

13. **Which two of the following would be defined as investment advisers under the USA?**
    I.   an economics professor with an active consulting business providing regular advice to
           pension funds as to which money managers to retain for the fund
    II.   a federal or state-charted bank
    III.   a property & casualty insurance company
    IV.   a lawyer who frequently advises non-accredited investors as to the value or advisability
           of investing in particular securities
    A.   I, II
    B.   I, IV
    C.   II, III
    D.   II, IV

14. **Which of the following persons would be defined as broker-dealers in the state?**
    A.   an agent selling promissory notes maturing in more than 12 months
    B.   a bank selling products insured by the FDIC
    C.   a firm with no office in the state that effects transactions with 7 pension funds in the
          state
    D.   a firm with no office in the state that effects 17 transactions with non-accredited
          investors who are residents of the state

15. **Which two of the following are securities?**
    I.   variable annuity
    II. fixed annuity
    III. whiskey warehouse receipt
    IV. commodity futures contract
    A.   II, IV
    B.   II, III
    C.   I, III
    D.   I, IV

16. **In which of the following instances has a sale been made?**
    A.   an investment representative offers variable annuities to several individuals
    B.   an individual makes an actual gift of non-assessable stock
    C.   a partnership makes an actual gift of assessable stock
    D.   a fiduciary pledges shares of NASDAQ stock as collateral to secure a loan for a client

17. **In which of the following cases has an investment representative sold a security?**
    A.   an agent of a broker-dealer donates convertible preferred stock to a tax-exempt foundation
    B.   a broker-dealer sells common stock to an individual client
    C.   an agent sells a client a fixed annuity
    D.   an agent sells a client a whiskey warehouse receipt

18. **The Administrator may do all of the following except**
    A.   issue injunctions
    B.   investigate outside the state
    C.   enforce subpoenas from out-of-state Administrators
    D.   require testimony even over 5th Amendment objections

19. **The Administrator may do all of the following except**
    A.   publish violations
    B.   publish denial orders
    C.   publish revocation orders
    D.   sentence violators to 3 years in prison

20. **The Administrator would have authority in all of the following cases except**
    A.   offer to sell originated in the state
    B.   offer to sell was directed into the state
    C.   payment for securities was made from the state
    D.   acceptance of an offer to sell was made in the state

21. **All of the following Administrative orders usually stem from unethical practices in the securities business except**
    A.   denial
    B.   revocation
    C.   suspension
    D.   cancellation

22. **All of the following orders require prior notice, opportunity for hearing, and written finding of fact and law except**
    A.   denial
    B.   revocation
    C.   suspension
    D.   summary suspension of a pending registration

23. **All of the following orders require prior notice and opportunity for hearing except**
    A.   stop order
    B.   denial
    C.   cease and desist
    D.   revocation

24. **All of the following can lead to denial, revocation or suspension except**
    A.   an individual indicates that she has an MBA from Northwestern University on her application, when, in fact, she has a BA from Northeastern University
    B.   an individual has been convicted of a non-securities-related felony 8 years ago
    C.   an individual has been convicted of a non-securities-related misdemeanor 2 years ago
    D.   the agent is insolvent

25. **All of the following can lead to denial of a registration except**
    A.   the individual is insolvent
    B.   the broker-dealer was enjoined by a court five years ago
    C.   the individual lacks experience in the securities business
    D.   the broker-dealer was subject to adjudication 7 years ago under federal securities law

26. **Which of the following is/are true concerning criminal penalties under the USA?**
    A.   there is no statute of limitations for securities fraud
    B.   the statute of limitations for securities fraud is 2 years from discovery or 3 years from the alleged event
    C.   ignorance of the law/rule has no bearing in criminal proceedings
    D.   the maximum penalty is 3 years in jail, $5,000 fine or both

27. **Which of the following companies will most likely use qualification to register their securities for sale in the state?**
    A.   XYZ Corporation, which plans to effect an IPO in all 50 states
    B.   ABC Corporation, which plans to effect an IPO in the state of Kentucky
    C.   GE, a listed company, plans to effect an additional offering of securities in all 50 states
    D.   MSFT, a NASDAQ company, plans a rights offering in all 50 states

28. **Which of the following is/are true statements concerning securities offerings in a state?**
    I.   the Administrator must be informed of all states where the security will be offered
    II.   the Administrator must be informed of the total amount of securities offered in all states
    III. the Administrator must be informed of the total amount of securities offered in the state
    IV.   securities offered by qualification or coordination may be placed in escrow and proceeds impounded until the issuer receives the specified amount
    A.   I, II, III, IV
    B.   I, III, IV
    C.   I, III
    D.   II, IV

29. **If a company plans to register their securities by filing, all of the following may be required except**
    A. a statement as to the company's eligibility for registration by filing
    B. no failure to make a debt payment or preferred dividend payment
    C. securities trading no less than $5 per share
    D. company must be in continuous operation for 39 consecutive calendar months

30. **All of the following methods of securities registration would lead to an effective date concurrent with federal except**
    A. filing
    B. notice filing
    C. coordination
    D. qualification

31. **Which of the following securities would most likely be subject to registration requirements at the state or Blue Sky level?**
    A. stock listed on NYSE
    B. stock listed on AMEX
    C. NASDAQ Small Cap Issue
    D. Non-NASDAQ stock

32. **All of the following are federal-covered securities except**
    A. GE
    B. MSFT
    C. Commercial paper maturing in 270 days
    D. OTC Bulletin Board stock

33. **All of the following persons are investment adviser representatives except**
    A. individual employed by a federal covered adviser who determines recommendations for clients
    B. individual selling the advisory services of a federal covered adviser
    C. individual performing clerical work for an investment adviser
    D. person supervising those who sell the services of an advisory firm

34. **A federal covered adviser must do all of the following except**
    A. pay fees to the state
    B. submit a consent to service of process
    C. provide notice to the state
    D. submit to surprise inspections by the Administrator

35. **In which of the following cases has an agent committed a fraudulent act?**
    A. an agent intentionally and willfully omits an immaterial fact to avoid distracting a client when offering a non-exempt security
    B. an agent intentionally omits an immaterial fact to avoid distracting a client when offering an exempt security
    C. an agent, knowing his client's distaste for companies without earnings, while offering XYZ stock indicates to the client that XYZ corporation, a small manufacturer in Ohio who failed to achieve positive earnings the past two years has, in fact, reported positive earnings every year of its existence
    D. an agent unwittingly accepts an unsolicited order for an unregistered, non-exempt security

36. **All of the following are prohibited practices except**
    A. a customer has refused to provide information on her financial situation, needs, and investment objectives. The investment representative recommends municipal bonds to the client, based on the prima facie evidence that the woman wore expensive jewelry and drove a foreign sports car to their last meeting
    B. an agent feels it is likely that a company like GRZ will be NYSE-listed and so she indicates to her clients and prospects that GRZ is a listed company
    C. an investment adviser takes custody of client funds in the absence of a rule against custody, informing the Administrator in writing
    D. an investment adviser representative tells a prospect that she has been approved by the Administrator to provide both technical and fundamental analysis on NYSE-listed securities

37. **Which of the following activities are prohibited?**
    I.   A long-standing non-discretionary customer of an investment representative has been purchasing REITS at least once a month over the past 10 years. On Monday, the client is not reachable by phone, so the representative buys 200 shares of Great Lakes REIT for the client, representing the minimum number of shares purchased by the client on any transaction over the past 10 years
    II.   An agent, after the customer indicates the number of shares to be purchased of a certain security, decides the time of day to buy the shares, even though the agent lacks discretionary authority
    III. Because a client is skeptical and hesitant about buying 1,000 shares of XYZ, the investment representative offers to act as a partner on the trade, splitting the gains or losses 60/40 with the client
    IV.   A husband and wife each have accounts with the same broker-dealer. The wife is too busy to get to the phone, so the husband calls and asks an agent of the broker-dealer to sell 500 shares of ORCL from the wife's account. The agent completes the transaction
    A. I, II, III, IV
    B. I, II, III
    C. I, III, IV
    D. II, III

38. **Commissions charged at Bobby Brown Broker-Dealers are normally $45 per trade. Recently, JoAnn Jackson was charged a commission of $75 for purchasing 1,000 shares of XYZL securities, which trade regularly on the OTC Bulletin Board. Which of the following statements are true of this situation?**
    I.   This is a fraudulent activity, punishable by five years in jail and a $3,000 fine
    II.   The higher commission must have been disclosed to Ms. Jackson before effecting the transaction
    III. Ms. Jackson must have given her consent to the higher commission rate before effecting the transaction
    IV.   Bulletin Board stocks should involve lower, not higher, commissions and/or markups
    A. I, IV
    B. II, III
    C. II only
    D. I, II

39. Your client has become fearful that XYZ common stock could plummet over the next several days. You are convinced that XYZ is a solid company about to report higher earnings, so when the client tells you to sell out the position, you over-ride her decision, based on the suitability information obtained on the new account form, and decide not to sell the security. What is true of this situation?
    A.   this is an acceptable practice based on accurate use of suitability information
    B.   this is a prohibited activity
    C.   this is a fraudulent activity
    D.   this is an example of trading on material inside information

40. All of the following statements by investment representatives are unacceptable except
    A.   "Treasury Bills are riskless securities guaranteed by the U.S. Government."
    B.   "Treasury Notes are riskless securities guaranteed by the U.S. Government."
    C.   "Treasury Bills are guaranteed by the U.S. Government, but do retain interest rate risk."
    D.   "If you invest in the Long-Term Treasury Mutual Fund right now, you can benefit by receiving the upcoming dividend."

41. All of the following activities by an investment adviser are prohibited except
    A.   entering into a contract that clearly states compensation shall be a percentage of capital gains
    B.   entering into a verbal contract with a client
    C.   entering into a contract with a customer that clearly discloses services, terms, fees, whether discretionary or non-discretionary, and the fact that no assignment of contract is allowed without written client consent
    D.   disclosing the identity, affairs or investment of a client to a third party without consent of client or court order

42. Which of the following is a true statement concerning broker-dealers?
    A.   states may require higher minimum capital requirements than federal
    B.   all broker-dealers must post fidelity/surety bonds
    C.   financial requirements must be paid in cash
    D.   all broker-dealers with custody and/or discretion must meet certain capital requirements and/or post fidelity/surety bonds

43. None of the following persons are agents except
    A.   an individual representing the City of Chicago in selling Chicago Revenue Bonds
    B.   an individual representing a broker-dealer selling Chicago Revenue Bonds
    C.   an individual working for Microsoft ® accepting unsolicited orders from the public
    D.   an individual representing Microsoft ® in transactions with underwriters

44. Which of the following persons are not agents?
    A.   an individual selling exempt securities for a broker-dealer
    B.   an individual selling IBM® stock to IBM® employees for which a small commission is received
    C.   a partner or officer of a broker-dealer who effects sales
    D.   an individual representing the Government of Montreal, Canada in selling Montreal revenue bonds to retail customers

45. Which two of the following Administrative orders most likely indicate that a person has performed an unethical act in the securities business?
    I.   denial
    II.   cancellation
    III.   withdrawal
    IV.   revocation
    A.   I, II
    B.   II, III
    C.   I, IV
    D.   II, IV

46. A customer was sold an unregistered, non-exempt security. What is true of such instances?
    I.   the customer is entitled to recover the amount paid for the advice and securities, plus court costs, reasonable attorney fees, and an unspecified amount for pain and suffering
    II.   the customer is entitled to recover the amount paid for the advice and securities, plus court costs, reasonable attorney fees, interest, minus any dividends/interest received from the securities
    III.   the customer may not sue if the advice was rendered by a federal covered adviser
    IV.   the customer may not sue if she has known of the illegal nature of the sale for 25 months
    A.   II, IV
    B.   I, IV
    C.   II, III
    D.   I, III

47. Which of the following are true statements concerning civil liabilities under the USA?
    A.   after receiving a written offer from the seller, the buyer may not sue if no action taken within 15 days
    B.   the Administrator's ruling on the matter is final and binding on the plaintiff
    C.   if the plaintiff dies, his/her children are prevented from pursuing the matter
    D.   the buyer is entitled to recover the price paid for the security/advice plus interest less any dividends/interest received

48. Karen Crenshaw discovers on April 10, 2001 that she was sold an unregistered, non-exempt security back on March 3rd, 1999. It is now July 3rd, 2003 and therefore
    A.   Karen still has the remainder of five years to pursue the matter before the statute of limitations precludes civil action
    B.   Karen may not sue the advisory firm at this point
    C.   Karen still has three years to pursue the matter before the statue of limitations precludes civil action
    D.   Karen still has the remainder of two years to pursue the matter

49. All of the following are defined as securities under the USA except
    A.   a certificate representing a 19% interest in a prize-winning thoroughbred
    B.   a certificate of 15% ownership of 1,000 head of cattle
    C.   a collateral trust certificate
    D.   a fixed annuity

50. The Sheriff of Macon County has seized the assets of local drug dealer and ne'er-do-well Billy Ray Roberts. Billy Ray's assets to be liquidated at the upcoming barbecue and asset liquidation party in Macon County include three Corvette® convertibles, several dozen vintage collectible firearms, and a sizable portfolio of stocks and bonds. With whom must the securities be registered before liquidation proceedings commence?
    A. administrator
    B. SEC
    C. NASD
    D. none of the above

51. What is true of a consent to service of process?
    I. if a registered person violates any provisions of the USA, actions against that person may commence by the service of process upon the Administrator
    II. only the most ethical professionals may obtain such consent to service of process
    III. it may be used in lieu of a fidelity/surety bond
    IV. filing the consent to service of process is equivalent to appointing the Administrator as the person's true and lawful attorney upon whom may be served all lawful process in any action against the person
    A. I, IV
    B. II, III
    C. II only
    D. III only

52. If a broker-dealer or investment adviser can not be located, the Administrator will most likely issue which of the following orders?
    A. revocation
    B. withdrawal
    C. suspension
    D. cancellation

53. If an applicant files a withdrawal, the withdrawal becomes effective
    I. as soon as the Administrator orders
    II. no later than 30 days after filing
    III. provided no revocations are pending
    IV. provided no suspensions are pending
    A. I, III
    B. II, III
    C. I, IV
    D. I, II, III, IV

54. Which of the following represents a violation of the USA?
    A. an agent shares commissions with other registered agents at the firm
    B. accepting an unsolicited order for an unregistered, non-exempt security
    C. soliciting orders for unregistered, non-exempt securities
    D. taking custody of client funds in the absence of a rule prohibiting custody

55. **An investment representative took a leave of absence from her broker-dealer employer in order to complete a 3-year MBA program. Now that the degree has been completed, the investment representative may**
   A.   return to work at the broker dealer provided that her license was properly parked at the firm during her absence
   B.   return to work at the broker-dealer provided that she earned her degree from an accredited university
   C.   not return to work without posting a surety bond for $75,000
   D.   not return to work as an investment representative before completing required licensing exams

56. **Which of the following is a true statement?**
   A.   a person who has operated as a broker-dealer for three years is automatically qualified to operate as an investment adviser
   B.   an individual who has five years' experience as an agent is automatically qualified to operate as an investment adviser
   C.   if the Administrator grants a broker-dealer a license, he/she has, in effect, also granted an investment advisory license to that firm
   D.   if the Administrator determines that a broker-dealership is not qualified to operate as an investment adviser—even though the firm has three years' experience as a broker-dealer—the Administrator may condition the applicant's registration as a broker-dealer upon their not transacting business in this state as an investment adviser

57. **Which of the following is a true statement concerning summary suspension of a pending registration?**
   A.   the Administrator may not summarily suspend a pending registration until the applicant has had an opportunity for hearing
   B.   an applicant whose pending registration has been summarily suspended must request a hearing within 15 days of receiving notification
   C.   when the Administrator summarily suspends a pending registration, the applicant must be notified promptly and informed that if a hearing is requested in writing, it shall be granted within 15 days after the receipt of the request
   D.   only a court of law can summarily suspend a pending registration

58. **A retail customer was sold a security by an investment representative who told her that XLU, Inc. had reported increased earnings the past 8 consecutive fiscal quarters, when, in fact, XLU had reported net losses in 3 of the past 5 quarters. What is true of this situation?**
   A.   it was a fraudulent sale and the customer may sue to recover the amount paid for the security, plus interest, less any income received from the security
   B.   it is not prohibited if the security is exempt
   C.   it is not prohibited if the transaction is exempt
   D.   it was fraudulent, but the customer may not sue if she no longer has the security in her possession

59. **All of the following transactions are exempt except**
   A.   an offer and sale of securities to 17 pension funds and 10 non-accredited investors in the state who buy for investment purposes and for which no commissions are paid by non-accredited buyers
   B.   a Marshall liquidates a drug dealers' securities at a public auction
   C.   a receiver in bankruptcy liquidates an insolvent company's portfolio
   D.   an investment adviser sells listed securities to several high net worth individuals

60. **Which of the following is a true statement concerning investment advisory firms established as partnerships?**

    A.   if a partner with a minority interest withdraws from the partnership, assignment of contract has occurred in violation of the USA

    B.   if a partner with a minority interest withdraws from the partnership, customers do not need to be informed

    C.   if a partner with a minority interest withdraws from the partnership, customers need to be informed

    D.   if a partner with a majority interest withdraws from the partnership, assignment of contract has not occurred

ANSWERS TO PRACTICE FINAL 2

1.   ANSWER: A

EXPLANATION: the question provides its own explanation, more or less. Just remember that the 12 b-1 fee can't exceed .25% (25 basis points) of "average net assets" if the fund wants to call itself "no-load." So "A" is okay—"B" is not. If the fee is equal to 25 basis points, fine. If it's greater than that, don't call the thing "no load." If there is a front-end load, the customer needs to be made aware of features that could reduce that load. Features like LOI's and breakpoint schedules must be pointed out to the customer. Should you have memorized that? No. The idea here is to sort of train yourself to know what is and isn't considered acceptable. "C" and "D" are supposed to sound somehow wrong to a careful and prepared test taker. If so, you could probably choose between A and B. If there is a problem with a 12 b-1 fee being called "no load", wouldn't it be more likely that a higher fee would cause the problem?

from "Dishonest or Unethical Practices . . .in connection with Investment Co. Shares"
http://www.nasaa.org [search the Library for Adopted Statements of Policy]

2.   ANSWER: D

EXPLANATION: yield is just income distributions divided by POP. Never include capital gains in that and be real clear with your customer about the difference between income distributions and total return. If you say that something is guaranteed against default risk, you can't just leave it at that. The customer might think there's no risk—there is risk. Interest rate risk will hit a government bond just as hard as a corporate bond. Interest-rate risk just means that when rates go up, debt security prices go down. And if you compare something to a CD or other insured bank deposit, you have to point out the thing you're comparing isn't guaranteed/insured the way a CD or other bank deposit is. Otherwise, it's not a fair comparison.

from "Dishonest or Unethical Practices . . .in connection with Investment Co. Shares"
http://www.nasaa.org [search the Library for Adopted Statements of Policy]

3.   ANSWER: D

EXPLANATION: remember not to combine capital gains with income distributions when calculating yield. Yield is just like for any exchange-traded or OTC share of stock: annual dividend distributed divided by price paid for the stock. What do I get divided/compared to what I paid to get it? That's yield. Capital gains is a whole nuther thing, and since you see how confusing the difference can be, imagine how the average investor could be misled if the registered representative wasn't real careful and thorough when discussing these terms. No projections allowed. The 1-, 5- and 10-year choices were a trick. Funds publish PAST returns for those periods, but NEVER predict future returns for any period, period. Regulators don't like agents putting customers into a bunch of mutual funds from different families, especially when the funds all hold the same basic portfolio and use the same basic investment approach. That would generate unnecessary loads and annual expenses paid right out of the investor's pocket.

from "Dishonest or Unethical Practices . . .in connection with Investment Co. Shares"
http://www.nasaa.org [search Library for Adopted Statements of Policy/Model Rules]

4. ANSWER: B

EXPLANATION: sounds goofy, but "no-load" funds usually do involve 12 b-1 fees that cover the same distribution expenses (printing, advertising, mailing, selling) that sales loads cover. They can still call themselves "no-load" as long as the 12 b-1 fee doesn't exceed .25% of average net assets. What's with the "12 b-1," by the way?

If you have your copy of the Investment Company Act of 1940, just look up section 12 b-1, and you'll see where it comes from.

For choice "A" remember that the prospectus has to be delivered, but that isn't the sum total of the representative's and firm's requirement to disclose material information. In most cases, the prospectus will probably cover what the investor wants to know, but if you know more material facts, you have to provide them. Again, NO PROJECTIONS/predictions allowed for mutual fund performance.

from "Dishonest or Unethical Practices . . .in connection with Investment Co. Shares"
http://www.nasaa.org [search Library for Adopted Statements of Policy/Model Rules]

5. ANSWER: C

EXPLANATION: not surprising that the firm has to first authorize all communications their rep's make about products/services provided by the firm. "C" is the answer because the order does not apply equally to

Federal Covered advisers. The deal with federal covered advisers is basically this: they have to pay a fee to the state and file a consent to service of process, as well as show the state the same stuff they showed the SEC. After that, they are really only going to bump into the Administrator if they appear to be engaging in fraud. *__Nobody__* is exempt from antifraud regulations of the State Securities Administrator, not even the State Securities Administrator. So, the federal covered advisory firm will only have to pay their "dues" so to speak to the state. As long as they watch their p's and q's, they won't really have to worry about the Administrator, or his/her little interpretive orders, releases, blah, blah, blah. They've already got the SEC watching them, which is enough to deal with all by itself.

from Interpretive Order Concerning Broker-Dealers, Investment Advisers, Broker-Dealer Agents and Investment Adviser Representatives Using the Internet for General Dissemination of Information on Products and Services

http://www.nasaa.org "Library"

6. ANSWER: A

EXPLANATION: the Administrator has power over ANYONE who commits fraud in his/her state. A firm or security might be registered at a higher level, or even excluded from registration at a higher level, but nobody—nobody—is exempt from antifraud regulations at the state level. Even though the advisory firm is "federal covered," it must still file a consent to service of process, which means if the firm gets in trouble the aggrieved party can serve court papers on the Administrator, who in this sense is acting as the firm's duly appointed attorney to accept service of process. In other words, once the consent to service of process has been filed, that firm or individual will not be able to escape court processes by fleeing the state. If the party can't be located to accept service of process, the aggrieved party will just serve the papers on the Administrator, which is just as good as serving them directly on the firm or individual in hot water.

Pretty clear that choice "IV" was false, right? Remember that advisers are fiduciaries, meaning they must put the needs of their clients ahead of their own. Not the same with agents/brokers/registered rep's. Them folks really represent the FIRM. They have to be ethical when dealing with the customer, but they really represent the firm. Not quite as high a standard in that sense.

From "NASAA Adopted Model Rules .. . Unethical Business Practices of Investment Advisers"

7. ANSWER: D

EXPLANATION: memorize it

From "NASAA Adopted Model Rules . . . Unethical Business Practices of Investment Advisers"

8. ANSWER: D

EXPLANATION: this practice is NOT illegal in all cases. Some states allow, some don't. The adviser checks to see if the state (the Administrator) has a problem with it. If not, the adviser may take custody as long as he/she/they inform the Administrator in writing that they now have custody of client securities/funds. At least once per year there must be a SURPRISE inspection, not a scheduled inspection. If the adviser knows it's coming, it's not much of an inspection, right? The account statements must be sent quarterly, not monthly—just something more to memorize.

From NASAA Adopted Model Rule "Investment Adviser Net Worth/Bonding Rule"

9. ANSWER: A

EXPLANATION: memorize it

From NASAA Adopted Model Rule "Sale of Securities at Financial Institutions"

10. ANSWER: C

EXPLANATION: if the firm has no office in the state, it can deal with 5 non-accredited/non-institutional investors and as many institutional—pension fund, mutual fund, insurance company, etc.—investors as they want.

Once you see they have an office in the state, though, you know they're always going to be defined as investment advisers, except when they aren't, like in choice "D." If they restrict their advice to only U.S. Government obligations, they're excluded from the definition of "investment adviser" completely.

If their only clients are investment companies, they go straight to the SEC/federal covered level. If their only clients are insurance companies, they are exempted at the federal level, which makes them federal covered by exclusion. And there is even a "local area adviser" exemption. If all clients are in the state, and no advice is rendered on exchange-listed securities, they are exempt from registration at the state/USA level.

Aren't you glad you know this? The test will be real glad if you know it, too.

11. ANSWER: D

EXPLANATION: they're a "person" as long as they're not a minor, dead, or declared mentally incompetent by a court of law—as opposed to a former spouse.

12. ANSWER: D

EXPLANATION: this one was tricky. If the individual representing GE receives commissions or is hired primarily/specifically to do this work, he/she is defined as an agent of the issuer and must register. If he/she does NOT receive commissions and is not hired primarily to do this activity or to skirt the USA, he/she is NOT defined as an agent and does NOT have to register. Choices "A" and "C" can be eliminated as soon as you see the word "broker-dealer." Broker-dealers are never agents, and agent are never broker-dealers. The third baseman sure isn't the right fielder, and under no circumstances shall the right fielder be the third baseman kind of thing. In choice "B" you see the individual represents an issuer, so you have to go through the whole flow chart—if you can find an exemption like an "unsolicited transaction," then the individual escapes the definition of "agent" and would not have to be sitting here reading this kind of junk, worrying about passing some required license exam.

13. ANSWER: B

EXPLANATION: pure evil on my part here. Often teachers and lawyers are NOT defined as advisers, but that's only if the advice is incidental to/not an integral component of their services. In choice "I" and "IV" both professionals are clearly providing advice, and even if you disagree, what choice do you have with the four cards you've been dealt? Play your hand wisely; never waste time quibbling with a test question. No time for that on the Series 63 exam.

14. ANSWER: D

EXPLANATION: choices "A" and "B" can be eliminated since B/D's are never agents or issuers. They're all separate players, like the pitcher, catcher, and first baseman. To choose between "C" and "D" just ask to whom they are performing transactions. If it's for any number of institutional investors (pension funds), they're not defined as being a B/D in the other state, but any more than 15 offers or transactions with non-accredited/non-institutional clients makes them a B/D in the other state.

Are we having fun yet?

15. ANSWER: C

EXPLANATION: if it's a "fixed" or guaranteed payment, it's NOT a security, so eliminate choice "II". Now you're sitting 50-50, which is a good place to be sitting when your guessing your little you-know-what off. Okay, now it's down to whiskey warehouse receipts and commodity futures. There aren't *that* many things to remember for what is NOT a security—not a commodity, a fixed payment, or precious metals. So, you have to like your odds here. Eliminate the commodity, or simply remember that something as bizarre as a "whiskey warehouse receipt" is, in fact, a security. If you really must know, when the distiller places the barrels of whiskey in a warehouse for storage, they receive a receipt whose value is backed up by the whiskey that will be aging for, perhaps, a decade or more. If they get impatient waiting on the whiskey, they can sell the whiskey warehouse receipt. Why would anyone buy it? It's called speculation, like a long-term option on the price of whiskey way out in the future. And if the paper turns out to be worthless, at least you can drink the whiskey, which is better than you can do with a piece of Enron paper, right?

Probably easier to memorize some of this stuff, rather than trying to understand *all* of it.

16. ANSWER: C

EXPLANATION: eliminate choice "A" because an "offer" is not a sale; it's merely an attempt to sell or the "solicitation of any offer to buy." Kind of sad that they have to write the law that way, but if they didn't, some scheister would get around making fraudulent sales by claiming he didn't try to sell anything—he merely tried to convince somebody to try to buy what he wasn't actually selling.

Not.

So an offer is both "an offer to sell" or "a solicitation of any offer to buy."

A sale is a "contract to sell or dispose of a security for value." Pledging is just pledging; it's not an offer or a sale, so eliminate choice D.

You're sitting 50-50 again. What do you remember about "assessable stock"? A "purported gift of assessable stock" is considered both an offer AND a sale. A gift of non-assessable stock is neither. So, eliminate choice "B", and you're left with "C".

17. ANSWER: D

EXPLANATION: you can eliminate choice "B" right off, since broker-dealers are not agents and vice versa. You can eliminate choice "A" when you see the words, "<u>donate</u> to a tax-exempt foundation." And, you can eliminate choice "C" because a FIXED annuity is NOT a security. Once again, you're left holding the whiskey warehouse receipt, which is, in fact, a security.

18. ANSWER: A

EXPLANATION: only a court can issue an injunction. The Administrator has to ask them, nicely. He/she/they can do the other three, though. They can make you talk, even over 5th Amendment objections, but they can't use the information you reveal against *you*. What if you don't talk? Your license ends up denied, suspended, or revoked, which is bad. And now you have to request a hearing, where you will—once again—be forced to talk to the Administrator.

19. ANSWER: D

EXPLANATION: that would also take a court, and, again, the Administrator would have to ask nicely.

20. ANSWER: C

EXPLANATION: nobody cares where payment is sent. The regulators get their authority to act when an offer is <u>directed from</u> or <u>into</u> their state, or an offer is <u>accepted</u> in their state. You're an agent in Ohio. You call an existing client driving through Arizona and try to sell her a stock. The offer originated in Ohio and was directed into Arizona, which gives both Administrators authority if any funny business takes place. If your customer hangs up and calls you back later from New Mexico and says she'll buy that stock, now the offer was accepted in New Mexico, and if anything funny takes place, the Administrator in New Mexico has authority. If the customer cuts the check while hiking in Colorado, nobody cares about that.

21. ANSWER: D

EXPLANATION: "cancellation" just means the person can not be located, no longer exists, or has been declared mentally incompetent by a court of law. If the person stopped sending in their renewal forms with the required fees, the state could cancel the registration, too. But, they only deny, suspend, or revoke when it's in the public interest, provides the public some form of protection, and the person did something really sneaky, stupid, or otherwise not a good idea.

22. ANSWER: D

EXPLANATION: if the registration is still pending, it can be summarily suspended even without prior notice and an opportunity for a hearing <u>prior</u> to entering that order (they get to request a hearing after the pending registration has been summarily suspended—not before that order is entered). The other three actions require what the stem of the question is stating.

23. ANSWER: C

EXPLANATION: it's like the principal of a school telling a suspected bully he has to go sit in the office a while because it looks like he might be thinking of hitting another kid later on in the day. Cease and desist. We'll sort it out later, but for now cease and desist. The other orders require prior notice and an opportunity for a hearing.

24. ANSWER: C

EXPLANATION: if the misdemeanor is not related to securities/money/ fraud, the individual can probably get his/her registration granted, but if it's a felony of any kind, no way. If the agent is insolvent, that can end up as a denial/suspension/revocation, and lying about credentials on the registration is a real bad idea all around.

25. ANSWER: C

EXPLANATION: if they didn't let newbies get started, how would anyone ever gain experience?

26. ANSWER: D

EXPLANATION: three years, five grand. "A" is false because there IS a statue of limitations—five years. "B" is false because that's the statute of limitations for civil liability, not criminal. And "C" is false because if the ignorant person can conclusively prove just how ignorant he/she was of the rule or order he/she violated, that person can not be sentenced to jail. Although they can be fined and made to wear a big, scarlet "I" on their lapels for a period of time prescribed by the Administrator.

27. ANSWER: B

EXPLANATION: you can see that XYZ, GE, and MSFT are all going inter-state, which is the jurisdiction of the SEC. So they have to register with the SEC. ABC will only deal with one state in their intra-state offering. So, they'll use qualification.

28. ANSWER: B

EXPLANATION: although some states actually DO want to know the total amount offered everywhere, your exam will say that the Administrator does not need to know that. So, you should tell the exam what it wants to hear, probably. What's the deal with "impounding proceeds?" Well, there's actually an adopted policy statement called "Impoundment of Proceeds" under NASAA's library. Not sure how far they'll go into that material, but you should know that some securities offerings have to be done through an escrow account where the proceeds are impounded (not released) until the issuer has raised what they said they were trying to raise. If they say they're raising $10 million and have only raised $1 million, the state isn't going to let them take the cash and walk away. The proceeds would be returned to the buyer's, plus interest earned in escrow, and the whole offering would be canceled.

Remember, the states don't like fly-by-night operations raising a little bit of money, grabbing the proceeds, and maybe fleeing the state.

29. ANSWER: D

EXPLANATION: it's 36, not 39, months.

30. ANSWER: D

EXPLANATION: qualification puts the issuer solely on the Administrator's turf. The other three are really dealing with the SEC and sort of keeping the Administrator informed, too. So those effective dates are always concurrent with federal . . . unless there are problems, like stop orders.

31. ANSWER: D

EXPLANATION: the other three are listed and/or NASDAQ, which gives them the "manual" or "blue chip exemption" and makes them "federal covered" securities.

32. ANSWER: D

EXPLANATION: GE is listed; MSFT is NASDAQ, and both are federal covered because of their "blue chip" exemption. That just means they deal with the SEC, which is plenty to deal with, by golly. The commercial paper is exempt at the federal level and, therefore, automatically exempt at the state level.

33. ANSWER: C

EXPLANATION: if the employee is doing "clerical/ministerial" work, that individual is excluded from the definition. But if they're selling the services of the firm or doing anything that smacks of analysis/money management— or supervising those folks who do that egghead stuff—them folks is all investment adviser representatives, even though they wish they weren't. I'm actually not sure what "ministerial" work is—I'm guessing it's stuff like filing, word processing . . . probably anything a "temp" would do. When—if—I track down the definition, I'll put it on the website.

34. ANSWER: D

EXPLANATION: choice "D" is going too far—it suggests that the federal covered adviser is under the jurisdiction of the Administrator, which it isn't. The adviser firm lets the state know they're in the state. They pay a fee, cause that always makes the states real happy. And they provide a consent to service of process because the Administrator has authority to enforce antifraud regulations on ANYONE. A "consent to service of process" means that an aggrieved party can just serve papers to/on the Administrator, which is just as good as serving them on the person/firm in trouble.

35. ANSWER: C

EXPLANATON: pretty clear that in choice "C" the agent is lying about material facts when offering securities. If that don't sound like fraud to you . . . well, I hope that DOES sound like fraud to you. In choice "A" and "B" the information was IM-material, so it should be omitted. In choice "D" the activity was unintentional. Prohibited, but not fraudulent. Intent is an important factor in criminal cases. Premeditated murder carries a much stiffer penalty than unintentional homicide. Either way, somebody's dead, but you're in much bigger trouble if you planned the murder rather than accidentally ran over a pedestrian while blabbing on a cellphone and slurping hot coffee.

    Right?

36. ANSWER: C

EXPLANATION: choice "C" describes exactly how an adviser should proceed when taking custody. No rule against it? Go ahead and take custody, as long as you inform the Administrator in writing. Choice "A" doesn't sound like an acceptable procedure, does it? The client could have rented the jewelry and the sports car, hoping to get preferential treatment from the firm. You need more tangible financial information than "she looked real rich" before recommending munibonds. In choice "B" remember that you can't tell somebody a stock will be exchange-listed when you really don't know one way or another. An in choice "D" remember the word "approved" should be a major red flag in any test question. The administrator didn't approve anything—he/she merely allowed the adviser rep to operate in the state and will suspend or revoke that privilege if he/she discovers the rep is using the dreaded a-word to clients and prospects.

37. ANSWER: C

EXPLANATION: in choice "II" the agent did nothing wrong, since time/price never equal discretion, anyway. In other words, you can always choose time or price, whether you have discretion or not. You just can't choose the action (buy or sell), the asset (which security), or the amount (# of shares) unless you have discretion.

For choice "I" the rep chose both the asset and the amount without discretion.

Oops.

In choice "III" the rep decided to violate the rule against "going halvsies" with a client. In choice "IV" the rep took an order from someone other than the client. Can't do that unless the other party has been granted "trading authorization" or "power of attorney."

38. ANSWER: B

EXPLANATION: do you see anything "fraudulent" here? Did anybody lie about anything? I see no evidence of deceit, so I would eliminate choice "I," which, in turn, eliminates choice "A" and "D."

Now, you're sitting 50-50, and you know choice "II" is in your final answer.

Don't "II" and "III" just seem to go together? Gotta give disclosure and get consent before charging higher commissions/markups.

Bulletin Board stocks, by the way, are funky and should involve higher markups. Think of a car dealer. The car dealer would give you a much better price if you're trading in a Toyota Camry® than if trading in a Pontiac Aztec®, right? They know there's a liquid/ready market for the Camry, whereas who the heck wants some funky vehicle in their inventory that doesn't know if it's a minivan, an SUV, or just a really ugly, impractical car?

MSFT or IBM would fetch a far better price than some funky stock nobody's ever heard of, right? So, markups on the illiquid stocks are higher to compensate for the risk of holding them in the dealer's inventory.

39. ANSWER: B

EXPLANATION: an agent can not deliberately refuse to sell a stock that the customer wants to sell. You can talk and cajole to the point of exhaustion, but if the customer wants to sell her stock, you have to sell it. Suitability information helps you RECOMMEND securities, but you aren't a fiduciary running a trust account, right? There's no deceit (fraud) or material inside information here, so "C" and "D" can be eliminated.

40. ANSWER: C

EXPLANATION: make sure the customer understands that Treasuries have no default risk but do carry interest-rate risk. Rates up—prices down, end of story. In fact, the long-term bonds have even more interest rate risk than short-term corporates.

Choice "D" is called "selling dividends," an offense punishable by firing squad as of September 1, 2002.

41. ANSWER: C

EXPLANATION: choice "C" is just a textbook explanation of what an investment advisory contract must include. Is there anything surprising about the information that must be included? If not, you sorta' haveta' choose that one.

Remember, you will be guessing your little you-know-what off on the day of the exam. That's why you have to try to eliminate answers that seem goofy to increase your odds, and go with the MOST LIKELY answer. You probably recall that capital gains is not the way to compensate an adviser, as it would skew their interests towards finding just one big winner and to hell with the rest of your portfolio. A "verbal contract"? No way—these advisory services are way too complicated to be stipulated in a "verbal contract," which wouldn't be worth the paper it wasn't written on. And, the adviser may NOT disclose their customer's business unless there's a subpoena/court order forcing them to do so, or the client says it's okay.

42. ANSWER: D

EXPLANATION: the financial requirements can be paid in cash or securities, usually Treasury securities. Because of NSMIA the states can never have a higher requirement than the feds. Not ALL B/D's post fidelity/

surety bonds—just the ones with custody/discretion. They either meet minimum net capital requirements, or they post a bond to cover the requirement and/or the shortfall.

43. ANSWER: B

EXPLANATION: you can't miss the lay-ups on this exam. You saw an individual representing a broker-dealer . . . that's your lay-up. Heck, if you're under 25 years old, that's your slam-dunk! If you missed this one, call me up so I can haze you mercilessly.

44. ANSWER: D

EXPLANATION: choices A-C were probably tempting, but if you looked at them hard enough, you saw that those folks were, in fact, agents. In choice "A" the individual represents a broker-dealer. In choice "B" the individual got a commission. In choice "C" the individual was effecting sales.

Is there any way you could argue that those folks ARE NOT agents?

No, so "D" has to be the answer. In choice "D" the individual represents an exempt issuer in the sale of exempt securities.

45. ANSWER: C

EXPLANATION: *cancellation* means the applicant no longer exists physically or mentally. Nothing punitive about cancellation. If you stopped using your credit card and the credit card issuer couldn't locate you, wouldn't they probably cancel your account? Doesn't mean you're in trouble; your account has simply been closed/canceled.

Same idea. Withdrawal means the applicant has changed her mind. Denial/suspension/revocation usually result from something unethical being done.

46. ANSWER: A

EXPLANATION: no "pain and suffering" is available. They get their money back plus interest, minus any dividends/interest received from the security. Federal covered doesn't mean the customer can't sue. The buyer can not sue if he/she has known about it more than two years. Or, if the seller makes a formal offer of rescission, the buyer can not sue if 30 days have passed and he/she has refused to accept the offer. In other words, at that point if they're going to sue they have to let the seller know where they stand.

47. ANSWER: D

EXPLANATION: cause of action goes on even after the death of the plaintiff or the defendant. Plaintiff = the one who's upset. Defendant = the one accused of upsetting the plaintiff. So the kids could still pursue the matter. There are civil courts where the plaintiffs can appeal the Administrator's ruling. And the buyer has 30—not 15—days before it's too late to sue.

48. ANSWER: B

EXPLANATION: the statute of limitations has kicked in: it's been more than 2 years from discovery.

    Sorry, Karen.

49. ANSWER: D

EXPLANATION: don't miss the lay-ups and/or slam-dunks. Fixed payments do NOT equal securities, so it's the "fixed annuity" you're looking for.

50. ANSWER: D

EXPLANATION: is the Sheriff of Macon County a securities dealer? Heck no. He/she is just gonna liquidate ole' Billy Ray's assets at the upcoming barbecue/asset liquidation party. If a fiduciary is liquidating assets and some of them-there assets are securities, that's an exempt transaction. As long as they're doing it in "good faith" and not trying to skirt the rules, the securities don't have to be registered. Sheriffs seize assets; US Marshals seize assets; receivers/trustees in bankruptcies seize and liquidate assets. If some of the assets turn out to be securities, that's okay. They don't have to be registered.

51. ANSWER: A

EXPLANATION: you don't "achieve" a consent to service of process—you just provide one. And when you do, an aggrieved party can serve papers on the Administrator, which is just as good as serving them on you. Ever read any John Grisham novels? Folks are often being told by tough-looking dudes, "Consider yourself served, buddy," and often ain't real happy about the message, which is why you usually wanna send a tough-looking dude to deliver it. A "consent to service of process" means you've already consented to let the Administrator receive "service" of court papers (subpoenas) just as if he/she is your lawful attorney. Of course, you might wanna then hire somebody more akin to Johnny Cochran for the actual hearing/trial, but you've still been served because somebody served papers on the Administrator. No reason at all to confuse this with a fidelity/surety bond, which is used to protect against theft/embezzlement.

52. ANSWER: D

EXPLANATION: we've already gone over this fascinating point.

53. ANSWER: D

EXPLANATION: if there are no Administrative actions pending (like deny/revoke/suspend), then the withdrawal is effective no later than 30 days after filing, or as soon as the Administrator says so.

54. ANSWER: C

EXPLANATION: "A" is okay. "D" is okay, as long as the Administrator is informed—if the question doesn't explicitly say the Administrator is NOT informed, don't assume he/she wasn't. So, you're down to "B" and "C".

    See the difference?

    If not, look again.

    Or give us a call/send us an email.

    As always, we're here to help.

55. ANSWER: D

EXPLANATION: boy, do the regulators hate that word "park"! No parking! If you're not working for a broker-dealer more than two years, you WILL have to take these exams again.

56. ANSWER: D

EXPLANATION: just something lifted directly from the Uniform Securities Act. Get yourself a copy . . . for real.

57. ANSWER: C

EXPLANATION: another good one to memorize. Lifted right out of the USA.

58. ANSWER: A

EXPLANATION: if a customer buys a security that was not properly registered for sale in the state, or if the seller offers/sells the security in a fraudulent manner, the customer may recover the amount paid for the security and/or advice, plus reasonable attorneys' fees and court costs, plus interest, minus any income received from the security. If the customer still has the security, she may "tender it to the seller," which is a fancy way of saying, "give the darned thing back to the jerk who sold it." Or, if the buyer has already dumped the thing, she may still recover amount paid, plus, etc. This is called a "rescission." Sometimes the seller realizes the error of his ways and makes an offer of rescission. Sometimes the seller is unrepentant and must be persuaded by the Administrator to make and follow through with an offer of rescission.

The Administrator can be very persuasive that way.

59. ANSWER: D

EXPLANATION: don't confuse a "federal covered security" with an "exempt transaction." A federal covered security simply has different registration requirements than those not federally covered. Review the list of exempt transactions, which includes sales by fiduciaries (sheriff, Marshall, Administrator, receiver), private placements (choice A), and several more.

60. ANSWER: C

EXPLANATION: two things going on with advisory firms structured as partnerships. If any member dies, withdraws or is admitted, customers must be informed. On a separate matter, if a minority partner dies, withdraws or is admitted, this does NOT constitute "assignment of contract."

Not sure why anyone ever thought it might, but it doesn't.

Unless it's a majority partner—then it does constitute "assignment of contract."

Hmm.

Whatever.

Practice Final 3

1. **Which of the following represents an acceptable sharing arrangement with clients?**
    A. an investment adviser shares the gains and losses in a joint account with a client after receiving written client consent
    B. an investment representative, after receiving client consent and approval from the branch manager, establishes a joint account with an immediate family member and shares the gains/losses/appreciation 60/40
    C. an investment representative shares the gains and losses of each transaction within a discretionary account
    D. an investment representative shares the gains and losses of each transaction within a non-discretionary account

2. **What is true of a securities offering completed via an Impoundment Agent?**
    A. if the proceeds are insufficient to meet the minimum requirements within the time prescribed by the Agreement, an affiliate or associate of the issuer may not purchase securities sufficient to meet the minimum requirements, even if such intentions are disclosed in the prospectus
    B. if the proceeds are insufficient to meet the minimum requirements within the time prescribed by the Agreement, the impoundment agent must release the proceeds directly to the Issuer
    C. if the proceeds are insufficient to meet the minimum requirements within the time prescribed by the Agreement, the impoundment agent must release the proceeds directly to the investors, plus a pro rata share of any interest earned on the proceeds
    D. if proceeds are insufficient to meet the minimum requirements within the time prescribed by the Agreement, the impoundment agent will deduct expenses from the proceeds or from the interest earned on the proceeds before releasing the proceeds to investors

3. **What is true of an Impoundment Agent?**
    A. an Impoundment Agent may be affiliated with the issuer
    B. an Impoundment Agent need not be domiciled in the United States
    C. an Impoundment Agent may be affiliated with the underwriters
    D. an Impoundment Agent must be a financial institution whose deposits are insured by the FDIC

4. **Anna Gomez worked for Adamson Broker-Dealers for three years. Now, she terminates her employment with Adamson to take a new job with Baker Broker-Dealers. Who must notify the Administrator?**
    A. Adamson Broker-Dealers
    B. Anna Gomez
    C. Baker Broker-Dealers
    D. all of the above

5.   **All of the following statements are true except**
     A.   options or warrants may be granted in connection with acquisitions, reorganizations, consolidations, or mergers
     B.   options or warrants granted in connection with acquisitions, reorganizations, consolidations, or mergers must be granted only to persons <u>affiliated</u> with the Issuer
     C.   options or warrants may not be granted in connection with acquisitions, reorganizations, consolidations, or mergers if the exercise price is less than 85% of fair market value of the Issuer's underlying shares of common stock on the date of the grant
     D.   the earnings of the Issuer at the time of the grant and after giving effect to the acquisition, reorganization, consolidation, or merger must not be materially diluted by the exercise of the options or warrants

6.   **The Issuer may grant options/warrants to an underwriter of a public offering of common stock. All of the following are true statements concerning this practice except**
     A.   the number of shares covered by underwriter's options/warrants does not exceed 10% of the shares of common stock actually sold in the public offering
     B.   the exercise price of warrants granted from Issuer to Underwriter must be at least equal to the public offering price of the common stock being offered to the public
     C.   the Issuer may grant warrants to the Managing Underwriter only
     D.   warrants granted by the Issuer to the Underwriter may be exercised within 120 days after the completion date of the public offering

7.   **A "promoter" of an issuer includes all of the following except**
     A.   an officer or director of the Issuer
     B.   anyone who legally or beneficially owns 5% or more of any class of the Issuer's equity securities
     C.   a person who receives 5% or more of the proceeds from the sale of any class of the Issuer's equity securities
     D.   an unaffiliated institutional investor who purchased the Issuer's equity securities more than one year prior to the filing date of the Issuer's registration statement

8.   **The Administrator may issue all of the following orders except**
     A.   stop
     B.   cease and desist
     C.   injunction
     D.   denial

9.   **A "promotional share" includes which of the following?**
     A.   equity securities issued by a promotional or development stage company to a promoter in exchange for cash
     B.   equity securities issued by a promotional or development stage company to a promoter for services rendered, patents, copyrights, and other intangibles
     C.   equity securities of an issuer that is not a promotional or development stage company issued in exchange for services rendered, patents, copyrights, and other intangibles three years prior to the filing of the registration statement
     D.   all of the above

10. **All of the following activities are prohibited by the USA except**
     A.   sharing commissions with other agents at the firm
     B.   pegging
     C.   capping
     D.   indicating that the Administrator has approved a security

11. **Which of the following are true statements concerning the Administrator's powers to grant or deny the registration of securities by an Issuer?**
    A. the Administrator does not have the power to deny a registration for an Issuer deemed to be in unsound financial condition
    B. the Administrator does not have the power to demand that an escrow account be established with proceeds impounded until the minimum amount is raised
    C. the Administrator may not deny the registration of a security due to excessive underwriter compensation
    D. a security's registration is effective for one year

12. **All of the following statements are true concerning the disclosure of risk factors in a prospectus or other disclosure document used in connection with an offering of securities except**
    A. the risk factors should be disclosed toward the end of the document
    B. the risk factor section should provide a succinct list of risk specific to the offering, with more detailed discussions of said risks clearly referenced to related sections of the body of the disclosure document
    C. risk factor disclosure alerts potential investors to all material risks involved in the offering that bear on the likelihood of business success and financial return to the investor
    D. risk factor disclosure protects the issuer from subsequent claims by investors that they were misled by the disclosure document

13. **An investment adviser may borrow money and securities from all of the following except**
    A. a broker-dealer
    B. a financial institution engaged in the business of making loans
    C. an affiliate of the adviser
    D. a client

14. **Which of the following are true statements?**
    I.   an adviser with custody of client funds/securities must maintain minimum net worth of $35,000
    II. an adviser with custody of client funds/securities whose minimum net worth falls below $35,000 must post bonds in the amount of the net worth deficiency rounded up to the nearest $5,000
    III. an adviser with discretion over a client's account who does not have custody of the client's securities/funds must maintain minimum net capital of $10,000
    IV. an adviser who accepts prepayment of $500 six or more months in advance must at all times maintain positive net worth
    A. I, II, III, IV
    B. I, III
    C. II, IV
    D. I, III, IV

15. **Which two of the following statements are true?**
    I.   if an investment adviser's net worth falls below the required level, the adviser must notify the Administrator within 5 business days of the deficiency
    II. after notifying the Administrator of deficient net worth, the adviser must file by the close of business on the next day with the Administrator a statement of financial condition
    III. "net worth" means the excess of liabilities over assets as determined by GAAP
    IV. an investment adviser is not deemed to be exercising discretion when it places a trade with a broker-dealer for a client who has signed a third-party trading authorization

with the adviser and whose advisory contract specifically states the adviser does not have discretion and, in fact, the adviser does not exercise discretion, and the client has signed a third-party trading agreement with the broker-dealer which specifically limits the adviser's authority to the placement of trades and deduction of advisory fees
A. II, IV
B. II, III
C. I, II
D. I, IV

16. **Broker-dealers operating on the premises of a financial institution where retail deposits are taken may use which of the following logo formats to provide sufficient disclosure in advertisements or sales literature?**
A. not FDIC insured
B. no Bank Guarantee
C. may Lose Value
D. all of the above

17. **Which of the following represent true statements concerning broker-dealers operating on the premises of a bank, savings & loan, or other financial institution?**
I.   wherever practical, the broker-dealer services shall be conducted in a physical location distinct from the area in which the financial institution's retail deposits are taken
II. in all cases the broker-dealer must clearly distinguish its services from the financial institution's retail deposit-taking activities
III. in those situations where physical space is limited, the broker-dealer may occupy the same physical space where retail deposits are taken, provided that the broker-dealer takes greater care to distinguish its services from those of the financial institution
IV. an arrangement whereby a broker-dealer operates on the premises of a financial institution taking retail deposits is referred to as a "networking arrangement"
A. I, II, III, IV
B. I, II
C. I, II, III
D. II, IV

18. **Which of the following statements are true concerning Internet communications?**
I.   a registered representative may not transmit information about securities products or individualized investment advice via the Internet if residents of states where the representative is not registered have access to the information
II. a registered representative may transmit information about securities products or investment advisory services available to residents of states in which the representative is unregistered so long as the Internet communication contains a legend that clearly states the representative may only transact business in states where he/she is licensed or excluded from licensing requirements
III. a broker-dealer or agent may transact business through the Internet with customers in states that the firm/agent are unregistered provided that the firm/agent is/are registered in the state where the primary DNS server is located
IV. the Internet communications of agents and advisory representatives must prominently disclose affiliation with the broker-dealer or investment adviser
A. I, II, III, IV
B. II, IV
C. I, III, IV
D. IV only

19. **Which of the following is a true statement concerning broker-dealers operating on the premises of a financial institution that takes retail deposits?**
    A. such an arrangement is illegal
    B. the broker-dealer may substitute "SIPC" in place of "FDIC" to explain that all products transacted by the B/D are insured
    C. the broker-dealer must disclose in oral and written form that products bought and sold through the B/D are not deposits or obligations of the financial institution
    D. none of the above

20. **All of the following are prohibited activities except**
    A. capping
    B. selling away
    C. front running
    D. arbitrage

21. **A registered representative receives a large order from an institution to purchase 20,000 shares of XYZT, a thinly traded Bulletin Board stock. Knowing the order will likely raise the price of XYZT, the registered representative astutely purchases 1,000 shares for the firm's own account before entering the large order. This practice is**
    A. a perfectly acceptable market arbitrage
    B. not prohibited when dealing with large, institutional orders
    C. a prohibited act known as capping
    D. a prohibited act known as front running

22. **A customer has granted discretion to her registered representative. The customer is in her early 60's and requires steady, monthly income. She is not willing to assume significant default risk. If the registered representative purchases high-yield corporate bonds, which TWO of the following are true statements?**
    I.   this represents a violation known as pegging
    II. this represents a violation known as abusing discretionary authority
    III. this would be referred to as an "unauthorized trade"
    IV. this is a fraudulent activity punishable by 5 years in prison
    A. I, III
    B. II, III
    C. I, IV
    D. II, IV

23. **An investment adviser is a sole practitioner/sole proprietor. When recommending trades, he will place transactions through XYZ Broker-Dealers, the firm paying him the most generous commissions. What is true of this practice?**
    A. it is fraudulent
    B. it is an example of misusing inside information
    C. customers must be informed of this potential conflict of interest
    D. it is a perfectly acceptable, time-honored practice in the advisory business

24. **As an investment adviser representative, you know that your clients are easily confused by excessive detail in the statements your firm sends to them. Your firm charges a wrap fee for the accounts that you manage. To avoid confusing your clients, you refer to the fee as a "commission". What is true of this practice?**
    A. it is unethical and prohibited
    B. it is not unethical if prior principal approval has been obtained
    C. it is unethical but not prohibited
    D. wrap fees are illegal post-2002

25. **XYZ Broker-Dealers distributes gifts of $250 to the top five producing registered representatives at the firm. This practice**
    A.   represents a fraudulent activity
    B.   represents a prohibited activity
    C.   does not represent a prohibited activity
    D.   is only allowable with prior SEC approval

26. **Why does the Administrator require that a consent to service of process accompany an application for registration?**
    A.   this distinction can only be achieved by federal covered advisors
    B.   it allows the Administrator to act as the applicant's attorney to receive service of court papers in non-criminal matters
    C.   NSMIA mandates the consent to service of process
    D.   This form acknowledges the applicant's consent to submit to urinalysis, polygraphs, and other recently mandated pre-qualification processes

27. **In which of the following cases was an offer to sell made in the state of Kansas?**
    A.   a newspaper published in Oklahoma announces that securities are available for sale
    B.   a newspaper published in Kansas, with 70% of the circulation outside Kansas, announces that securities are available for sale
    C.   after receiving an offer to sell in the state of Oklahoma, a customer drops a check for payment of the securities in a Kansas mail box
    D.   while driving through the state of Kansas, a customer receives an offer to sell from a registered representative, whose office is located in Missouri

28. **Failure to comply with an Administrative cease and desist order is known as**
    A.   contempt
    B.   contumacy
    C.   breach of contract
    D.   fraud

29. **Jennifer Johnson's application for a securities salesperson's license has been officially denied by the state securities Administrator. She may appeal this order**
    A.   if she works for a federal covered adviser
    B.   if she works for an exempt issuer
    C.   by filing an appeal in the appropriate court within 30 days
    D.   by filing an appeal in the appropriate court within 60 days

30. **An intrastate initial public offering is expected to last at least 120 days. How often must the issuer provide reports of sales to the Administrator?**
    A.   weekly
    B.   monthly
    C.   quarterly
    D.   once

31. **Banker's acceptances are exempt from registration requirements as long as all of the following characteristics are inherent except**
    A.   in one of the top three credit ratings
    B.   at least $50,000 denomination
    C.   maturity of 270 days or less
    D.   issued by a listed/NASDAQ company

32. **All of the following are exempt from state-level registration except**
    A. building & loan securities
    B. XLYZ, and OTC Bulletin Board stock
    C. Oracle® 5.25% convertible preferred stock
    D. T-bonds

33. **A transaction in pre-organization certificates would qualify for an exemption if**
    A. no subscriber makes any payment
    B. number of subscribers does not exceed 10
    C. no commission is charged/provided
    D. all of the above

34. **As long as the proceeds do not go to the issuer, it is okay to sell a limited number of outstanding unregistered, non-exempt securities per broker-dealer per year. This exemption is known as**
    A. fiduciary pledge
    B. isolated, non-issuer transactions in outstanding securities
    C. private placement
    D. underwriter transaction

35. **Which of the following persons will most likely have to register as an investment adviser?**
    A. broker-dealer
    B. agent
    C. certified financial planner
    D. accountant

36. **All of the following persons must register as investment advisers in the state except**
    A. an attorney with an office in the state who provides regular advice to pension funds as to which money managers to hire and retain
    B. a CPA with an office in the state who places an ad in the Yellow Pages® announcing that she provides investment advice on non-exempt securities
    C. an adviser with an office in the state whose only clients are insurance companies
    D. an adviser with no office in the state who directs communications to 8 non-accredited investors

37. **An agent is not registered in the state of Alabama. The agent sells a revenue bond issued by the State of Alabama to an Alabama resident. What is true of this case?**
    A. the practice is acceptable because municipal bonds are exempt securities
    B. the practice is acceptable because the bond was issued by the State of the customer's residence
    C. the practice is unacceptable because revenue bonds must be registered
    D. the practice is unacceptable because the agent must be registered in Alabama

38. **An Issuer shall be deemed to be in unsound financial condition if its financial statements contain a footnote or if the independent auditor's report contains an explanatory paragraph regarding the Issuer's ability to continue as a going concern in addition to which of the following conditions?**
    A. inability to meet current obligations as they come due
    B. negative cash flow
    C. negative shareholder equity
    D. all of the above

39. An investment adviser representative is responsible for landing new accounts for the firm for whom she works. 72 hours after landing a new account, she discloses to the client that she was convicted of a non-securities related misdemeanor three years earlier. What is true of this situation?
   A.   it is an act of fraud
   B.   it is a prohibited act
   C.   it is not a prohibited act because she disclosed the required information within 5 days
   D.   it is not a prohibited act because the misdemeanor was non-securities related

40. All of the following facts must be disclosed to advisory clients except
   A.   precarious financial condition of the advisory firm
   B.   legal or regulatory actions against the firm material to evaluation of the firm's integrity
   C.   whether the account is discretionary/non-discretionary
   D.   whether the Administrator permits custody

41. A customer has informed you, her agent, that her signed power of attorney has been mailed from a U.S. Post Office and gives a legitimate address of said post office. At this point, you may choose which of the following aspects of a transaction?
   A.   price
   B.   amount to be purchased/sold
   C.   security to be purchased/sold
   D.   all of the above

42. Which of the following facts will most likely cause a private placement to lose its exemption from advertising and filing requirements?
   A.   more than 10 accredited investors will be solicited
   B.   commissions are paid by non-accredited investors
   C.   more than 10 accredited investors will pay commissions
   D.   not all accredited investors are buying for investment purposes

43. Which of the following are true statements concerning underwriter compensation?
   A.   the Administrator may disallow an offering if the underwriting expenses exceed 17% of the gross proceeds from the public offering
   B.   underwriting expenses may include but are not limited to commissions to underwriters and broker-dealers, underwriter's warrants, and underwriter's due diligence expenses
   C.   an offering may be disallowed by the Administrator if the direct and indirect selling expenses of the offering exceed 20% of the gross proceeds from the public offering
   D.   all of the above

44. An Issuer may grant options and/or warrants to an unaffiliated institutional investor in connection with a loan provided that
   A.   the options/warrants are issued contemporaneously with the issuance of the loan
   B.   the exercise price of the options/warrants is not below the fair market value of the issuer's shares of common stock underlying the options/warrants on the date the loan was approved
   C.   the number of shares issuable upon exercise of the options/warrants multiplied by the exercise price thereof does not exceed the face amount of the loan
   D.   all of the above

45. **Which of the following methods of registration for securities will be effective as so ordered by the Administrator?**
    A.   notification
    B.   qualification
    C.   coordination
    D.   all of the above

46. **Which of the following is a true statement concerning civil liability?**
    A.   if the plaintiff is deceased, no action may be taken by the heirs
    B.   if the defendant is deceased, no action may be taken against the employing firm
    C.   if a security is sold by means of any material misstatement of fact, the seller may be forced to repurchase the security with interest less any income received from the security by the purchaser
    D.   the statute of limitations is 7 years

47. **Which of the following is a true statement concerning an applicant who requests review of an Administrative order to deny, revoke, or suspend?**
    A.   the appeal must be filed within 15 days
    B.   once the appeal is filed, the Administrative order is immediately stayed
    C.   the appeal must be filed within 60 days
    D.   the court may only alter the Administrative order; it may not set it aside

48. **A customer of a broker-dealer properly registered in Montana receives a phone call from a registered representative of the firm while the customer is driving across the Idaho panhandle. The representative offers convertible debentures to the customer, and the customer tells the representative he will consider the offer and call him back. Two hours later, while driving near Cheyenne, Wyoming, the customer calls the representative back and leaves a voice mail indicating that he will, in fact, purchase the securities offered. In Colorado, early the next morning, the customer drops a check in a U.S. Post Office drop-box. Where was the offer accepted?**
    A.   Montana
    B.   Idaho
    C.   Wyoming
    D.   Colorado

49. **Which of the following is defined as a "person"?**
    A.   individual with an IQ of only 110
    B.   minor
    C.   deceased individual
    D.   individual declared mentally incompetent by a court of law

50. **The Administrator for the State of Maryland has good reason to believe that a broker-dealer is about to offer unregistered non-exempt securities in a primary market transaction. Which of the following orders will most likely be issued?**
    A.   habeas corpus
    B.   cease and desist
    C.   injunction
    D.   revocation

51. **Which of the following would most likely be defined as securities?**
    I.   ownership of 10 racehorses
    II.   certificate of 10% ownership in one racehorse
    III. whiskey warehouse receipt
    IV.   term life insurance policy
    A.   I, II, III, IV
    B.   II, III
    C.   II, III, IV
    D.   I, II

52. **Which of the following represents a secondary market transaction?**
    A.   XYZ Corporation, which effected an IPO four years ago, is now offering additional shares to the public in a second offering of common stock
    B.   Jack Walsh, former CEO of ABC Corporation, left the corporation with 10,000,000 shares of unregistered, restricted stock. He is now hiring an underwriter to register the shares and offer them to the public
    C.   both
    D.   neither

53. **Which of the following statements concerning preferred stock is/are true?**
    I.   a public offering of preferred stock may be disallowed by the Administrator if the Issuer's adjusted net earnings for the last fiscal year were insufficient to pay its fixed charges and preferred stock dividends
    II.   a public offering of preferred stock may be disallowed by the Administrator if the Issuer's average net earnings for the last three fiscal years was insufficient to pay its fixed charges and preferred stock dividends
    III. the Administrator may use "Net Cash Provided by Operating Activities" from an Issuer's Statement of Cash Flows in lieu of Average Net Earnings to determine acceptance/denial of a preferred stock offering
    IV.   a public offering of equity securities may be disallowed by the Administrator if the Issuer's articles of incorporation authorize the board of directors to issue preferred stock in the future without a vote of common shareholders
    A.   I and III
    B.   I and II
    C.   II and III
    D.   I, II, III, and IV

54. **Which of the following represents a non-issuer transaction?**
    A.   initial public offering
    B.   subsequent primary offering
    C.   secondary offering
    D.   private placement

55. **In which of the following cases did an investment representative most likely commit fraud?**
    I.   an agent willfully omits an immaterial fact when offering securities to a retail client in order to keep the presentation focused and increase the likelihood of a sale
    II.   a client is convinced that she was offered and sold securities totally unsuitable for her investment needs
    III. an agent recommends a security based on material inside information
    IV.   an agent willfully solicits orders for an unregistered, non-exempt security
    A.   I, II, III, IV
    B.   III only
    C.   I, III only
    D.   IV only

56. All of the following business practices are prohibited. Which one is most likely fraudulent, as well?
- A. recommending securities on the basis of material, inside information
- B. misstating a material fact in the offer/sale of securities
- C. rendering unsuitable recommendations to a retail client
- D. commingling customer funds with broker-dealer funds

57. Your customer is a 58-year-old woman of substantial means. Her name is Barbara Bensen, and she enjoys golfing, tennis, cooking, and Scrabble®. Her dog's name is Minnie. Minnie is a spaniel-terrier mix. A good dog by all accounts. This morning Ms. Bensen comes into your office at XYA Broker-Dealership and informs you that she just read several negative analyst reports on QRT common stock. Ms. Bensen is convinced that the stock is about to plummet, and even after you spend a half hour trying to convince her otherwise, she insists that it is time to sell her 20,000 shares of QRT. So, you accept the order to sell 20,000 shares QRT but before placing such a large order you sell 300 shares of QRT out of your own account. What is true of this practice?
- A. it is acceptable only with prior principal approval
- B. it is acceptable provided that the customer sell order is placed within 90 seconds of your sell order
- C. it is a clear act of fraud
- D. it is prohibited, with or without principal approval

58. What do we call the person responsible for ADMINISTERing the USA in a state?
- A. Sir
- B. Ma'am
- C. Your honor
- D. ADMINISTRATOR

59. Which of the following Investment Advisers will have to register at the state level?
- A. a firm with an office in the state whose only clients are registered investment companies
- B. a firm with an office in the state whose only clients are insurance companies
- C. a firm with an office in the state whose advice relates only to Treasury securities
- D. a firm with no office in the state who services 9 non-institutional clients who are residents of the state

60. All of the following activities are prohibited except
- A. an investment representative recommends the same security to 135 clients because he thinks it's a can't-lose investment opportunity
- B. an investment adviser uses verbal contracts for clients with $100,000+ under management
- C. a trader buys shares of IBM for the firm's account at $80 on the NYSE while simultaneously selling it for $80.17 on the Chicago Stock Exchange
- D. a broker-dealer holds customer funds and securities together with the firm's account

Answers to Practice Final 3

1. ANSWER: B

EXPLANATION: investment advisers do NOT share in the gains/losses of their clients' accounts, so you can eliminate choice A. Broker-dealers don't really like registered reps (investment reps) sharing with clients, either. Only way to do it is to have an approved joint account at the firm, get the customer's consent, and share according to your contributions. If you put in $3,000 and your college buddy ponies up $30,000, you can not share things 50/50. When it's a family member, though, the sharing arrangement is up to you and your family member. The rep can't share per transaction, which would violate the no-going-halvsies rule. Discretion is meaningless in that case. Don't share per transaction—you'd have to set up a joint account. Good luck getting it approved.

2. ANSWER: C

EXPLANATION: if you got this one right, there are a few possibilities. You guessed wildly and got lucky. You actually read the NASAA Adopted Statement of Policy "Impoundment of Proceeds." Or, you just took the most likely sounding choice.

Not that you have to show your work on the Series 63. A right answer is a right answer.

Well, this one is so unlikely to show up on the exam, I'm not going to spend time explaining it. I actually sent an email to NASAA asking for more detail on "impoundment agent." One of the bigwigs there wrote back that he was not familiar with the term "impoundment agent." I told him to check their website for a statement of policy bearing that very term.

Well, if NASAA ain't familiar with the term, I don't think there's much of a chance they'll ask YOU about it.

Unless they do.

And then you'll be glad you saw this silly question.

3. ANSWER: D

EXPLANATION: memorize it and don't sweat it. I really can't see them asking about impoundment agents. Just remember that securities registered under coordination or qualification usually require an escrow account run by an escrow agent or an impoundment agent, who won't release the proceeds until the issuer/underwriters have raised the minimum amount they're trying to raise.

4. ANSWER: D

EXPLANATION: not a tough question at all. Both employers and the rep most notify.

5. ANSWER: B

EXPLANATION: you can read the NASAA statement of policy on "options and warrants" if you want. Seems only remotely possible to show up on the test. If it did, I could maybe picture a question like this one. Since B is false, you can see what would make it true—and the other three choices are all true. So take this one for what it's worth.

Not much.

6. ANSWER: D

EXPLANATION: the options/warrants can't be exercised for one year, not 120 days. The other three statements are true. This is from the adopted statement of policy "Underwriting Expenses & Underwriter's Warrants."

7. ANSWER: D

EXPLANATION: this comes from the "Corporate Securities Definitions" adopted statement of policy. Read it if you have the time.

8. ANSWER: C

EXPLANATION: only a court can issue an injunction, just as only a court can sentence you to prison.

9. ANSWER: D

EXPLANATION: also from the adopted statement of policy called "Corporate Securities Definitions," a publication only slightly more entertaining than a big city phone directory.

10. ANSWER: A

EXPLANATION: as long as the agent is connected with your firm and is registered, you can share commissions. Don't do the other three, though.

11. ANSWER: D

EXPLANATION: for the other three choices, just omit the word "not" to make it true. The Big A DOES have the power to deny a registration for securities sold by shaky companies. The Big A DOES have the power to demand an escrow account whose proceeds are not released until the minimum amount of $ is raised. And if the Big A thinks your underwriters are making too gosh-darned much money, he can deny the registration.

12. ANSWER: A

EXPLANATION: even if you haven't yet read the adopted statement of policy called "Risk Disclosure Guidelines," you could probably have guessed that the regulators want the risks disclosed UP front—not at the end of some long, boring document guaranteed to put most readers to sleep. And that, I feel, is one of the most important skills you must develop.

13. ANSWER: D

EXPLANATION: wouldn't "a client" be the most likely guess on your part? If not, sharpen your guessing skills.

14. ANSWER: A

EXPLANATION: I think this is more of a Series 65/66 question, but I can't bank on that. So, re-read the choices and file them away in memory somewhere. You can also read NASAA's Adopted Model Rule Investment Adviser Net Worth/Bonding Rule

15. ANSWER: A

EXPLANATION: this also comes from NASAA's Adopted Model Rule Investment Adviser Net Worth/Bonding Rule. Choice "I" is incorrect because the IA must notify by the close of the next business day, not within 5 days. And choice "III" has it exactly backwards, right? If your liabilities exceed your assets you have negative net worth. Net worth is assets in excess of liabilities, something most dot-com companies did not have, which is why they are no longer here. So, even though choice "IV" is slightly absurd, you could have gotten the right answer just by eliminating "I" and "III."

Use test-taking skills to the max!

16. ANSWER: D

EXPLANATION: you may have seen these very words on an advertisement at your local branch bank. I think you should read NASAA Adopted Model Rule "Sales of Securities at Financial Institutions". Just seems like a good topic to test.

Maybe.

17. ANSWER: A

EXPLANATION: all statements are true—memorize them and read the adopted Model Rule on Sales of Securities at Financial Institutions.

18. ANSWER: B

EXPLANATION: big difference between providing information on a securities product and actually selling that product, right? So, if you provide info on products to folks in states where you aren't registered, you have to make it clear that you can only sell to folks in states where you ARE registered. You must also prominently display your affiliation with your broker-dealer. I would also read the adopted statement of policy on Internet Communications (the title is too long to repeat).

19. ANSWER: C

EXPLANATION: this "networking arrangement" is not illegal; it's just carefully regulated. The B/D must make it real clear that their products are a whole new ball game compared to insured/guaranteed bank products. SIPC may NOT be substituted for FDIC, because it isn't the same thing at all. SIPC still leaves us with market risk.

20. ANSWER: D

EXPLANATION: arbitrage is okay. Not sure why the 63 wants you to know that, but go ahead and know that.

21. ANSWER: D

EXPLANATION: don't be doing any frontrunning if you can help it. The regulators hate it when you take advantage of a big order by buying the stock first, then letting the big buy order from a customer take the price up.

Yes, they do take all the fun out of this business.

22. ANSWER: B

EXPLANATION: pegging is market manipulation. You and I come up with a scheme to make it look like a bunch of trading in a thinly traded stock is going on, trying to raise the price a couple of *pegs* through clever and unlawful market manipulation.

But that's not what's going on in the practice question.

Whenever a rep has discretion and buys something unsuitable, we can consider that an abuse of discretionary authority, and the trades could be referred to as "unauthorized trades." The customer authorized the rep to buy things that were suitable. Unsuitable stuff, therefore, was not authorized. *Un*authorized.

23. ANSWER: C

EXPLANATION: it would be a conflict of interest if your recommendations could, on the one hand, lead to transactions that cost your clients much less than XYZ charges, or, on the other hand, cost your client more and put more money in your pocket.

Hmm. You'd like to help your client out, but you're kind of used to helping your wallet out, too.

A conflict of interest.

An IA is a fiduciary, who must put his clients' needs ahead of his own. If there's a conflict, whereby what's best for the customer might not be best for the IA and vice versa, the conflict must be disclosed.

And, don't be too quick to pull the "fraud" trigger. Not everything that seems shady is fraudulent. Fraud is the blatant, willful, knowing attempt to deceive another party in the purchase/sale of securities and/or investment advice. Your customer is morally opposed to tobacco stocks. You sell her 1,000 shares of Altria and swear that it's a "consumer products" company, not a tobacco company.

Whoah! Wait a minute now! Altria (Phillip Morris) has something like 50% of the U.S. cigarette market, plus huge chunks of the international market. They're the biggest tobacco company in the world—ever heard of Marlboro®? While they might own 80% of Kraft Foods®, and while cigarettes are technically a "consumer product," you know it's a deceitful answer, and you lied anyway in order to sell your customer some stock.

Fraud.

Here's the subtle difference between a prohibited act and an act of fraud:

Charging customers commissions that are way out of line is a prohibited act. It could get your firm's license suspended or revoked, which is bad. Charging commissions of $75 and telling customers you only charged them $25 . . . now that's not just prohibited; it's fraud!

See the difference?

They might not even force you to make the distinction, but if they do, remember that fraud is the willful attempt to deceive someone in the purchase or sale of securities and/or investment advice.

24. ANSWER: A

EXPLANATION: a "wrap fee" can only be charged by advisory firms/reps. A commission is for broker-dealers/agents. Investment Advisers charge fees for their advice. Since many also execute trades, they take the commission and the advisory fee and "wrap it altogether." They call the combined fee a "wrap fee," cause we never get real creative with the language in this business. An agent charges a commission. Only an adviser can charge a "wrap fee." Big difference—don't mislead the customer about the terms.

25. ANSWER: C

EXPLANATION: when you study for these tests, sometimes you start to suspect that just about *everything* is wrong. Well, don't go too far. A firm can give gifts and bonuses to their own employees. But a broker-dealer can't give more than $100 per year to other agents at other firms. They don't want people buying influence in the business. How much influence can you buy for $100 these days?

Not much, which is exactly how the regulators want it.

Why would a broker-dealer want to give other agents money? Maybe the B/D sponsors a mutual fund and makes a really nice selling concession on each share sold. Maybe they just want to spread their cash around to entice agents to focus on their mutual fund, not those 10,000 other funds out there.

26. ANSWER: B

EXPLANATION: that's exactly what this form does. Under "uniform forms" at www.nasaa.org you can actually download one of these. Might help to hold one in your hands, make it more tangible. It's a form that lets the Administrator receive legal papers on your behalf, in case somebody really wants to locate you when you really don't want to be located. You flee the state—no problem! The other party and the courts know exactly how to reach your "duly appointed attorney," the state Securities Administrator. In my state, it's the Secretary of State, someone well known by anyone with a driver's license. I could find that guy, no matter which cave you might be hiding in. I'd serve him the court papers, and now you've been served. Time to come on out of that cave now or face contempt of court charges, which is bad. Plus it makes you look like a malcontent when they try you for the alleged offenses that got you in hot water to begin with. The orange jumpsuit never does much for your credibility, either.

But I digress.

No state-mandated polygraphs or urinalysis that I know of—did you have to submit to those tests? I sure hope not.

Choice A was bogus—this a form that you sign, not a professional credential.

27. ANSWER: D

EXPLANATION: this type of question is highly likely to show up on your exam.

Lucky you.

Here's the deal. The USA says that the Administrator of a state has jurisdiction over an offer originating in his state, being directed into his state, or being accepted in his state. In choice D, the offer originated in Missouri and was directed into Kansas. So an offer was "made" in both states, really, and certainly in Kansas. So the Kansas Administrator definitely might have some say-so if anything funky goes down. As would the Missouri Administrator. The state where the check is dropped off isn't significant. It's where the offer to sell or "solicitation of any offer to buy" originates, is received in, or is accepted in. As a registered rep, you call me from your office in Ohio. I'm in Georgia using my cellphone. You try to sell me a mutual fund. So, an offer *originated* in Ohio and was *directed into/received* in Georgia. I'm skeptical and by the time I return your 7th frantic voice mail I'm in Biloxi, Mississippi. If I call you from Mississippi and say I'll buy that mutual fund, the offer has been *accepted* in Mississippi and that state's Administrator has jurisdiction if anything funky goes down, too. So now we better hope we're minding our p's and q's, because the Administrators of Ohio, Georgia, and Alabama might be able to make us sweat big time. If you have any doubts, go to the Ohio securities Administrator's website and check out all the past denials, suspensions, revocations, and cease and desists they've issued at www.securities.state.oh.us.

See how they love to name names? Imagine if *your* name were on any of those well-publicized administrative orders.

No thanks, right? That's the subtext of this whole thing called the Series 63. Don't mess around in this business or there *will* be consequences. We won't shoot you, but by the time we're done messing with you you'll wish we *had* kind of thing.

Choices A and B are based on one of the funkiest parts of the Uniform Securities Act. If the newspaper is published in Wisconsin and purchased by a reader in Illinois, who sees an ad for securities, that offer was NOT made in Illinois.

Not yet, anyway.

Actually, if the Illinois guy calls the number and says he'd like to buy some of them-there securities and—for the sake of argument we'll assume the other side says YES—now an offer to buy was made and accepted in Illinois. But, if nobody calls that number, no offer has been made in Illinois. It was "made" in Wisconsin, so if it's misleading the Big A in Wisconsin has jurisdiction.

And if you thought *that* was weird, they also decided that if a newspaper is published in Illinois but has 2/3 (66.7%) of its circulation *outside* Illinois, now a published offer to sell securities would NOT have been made in Illinois, but in the state where the customer sees the ad.

Wow, I really hope they cut you some slack on this concept, but I wouldn't bet on it. I have a feeling regulators think this is an important point about jurisdiction, which is what *they* care about. So, let's pretend *we* care, too. At least long enough to pass the test and move on with our lives.

28. ANSWER: B

EXPLANATION: **contumacy** is the act of disregarding an Administrator's order. You do that, and he's likely to take it to a judge, who will issue a court order. You blow that one off, and now you've committed **contempt** of court.

And that always ticks off the judge big time. In fact, now that you've shown your contempt for the court, guess what the judge, AKA "the court," is gonna' show you at your little trial?

Total contempt. All over your act of contumacy and subsequent bad attitude.

29. ANSWER: D

EXPLANATION: she has 60 days to file an appeal of the Administrator's order in the appropriate court of law.

30. ANSWER: C

EXPLANATION: the USA says the Administrator can not require progress reports more often than quarterly. Maybe it seems bizarre that it would take 120 days to sell all the newly issued securities. That's because we hear/read about the big IPO's, like Netscape, Krispy Kreme, or BlueJet. Many little offerings made by relatively unknown companies are subject to state jurisdiction/registration and can take months, years even. If so, the issuer has to tell the Administrator how many shares have been sold— how much money has been raised—but not more often than quarterly.

31. ANSWER: D

EXPLANATION: chances are, the company would be listed, or NASDAQ, but only the first three choices are <u>requirements</u>

32. ANSWER: B

EXPLANATION: the stock has to be exchange listed or part of NASDAQ'S National Market System. Bulletin Board/Pink Sheet stocks are NOT part of NASDAQ'S NMS. Ever had one of them funky tech stocks get booted off NASDAQ?

It goes to the security industry's equivalent of purgatory, the OTC Bulletin Board. There it pays for its sins by being jostled around mercilessly by frantic buyers and panic sellers, who often cause the stock to rise 20% one day only to crash and burn 35% the next.

Seldom do these stocks ever make it out of purgatory and back into that electronic paradise known as NASDAQ or the "National Market System".

So, these securities—these OTC BBN stocks—get no exemption from registration. If the exam says "penny stock," lump that in there, too, cause it's close enough for rock 'n' roll. As far as the other three choices, I'm sick of talking about them. You've read my spiel in the text or the earlier practice finals by now, and you're probably sick of hearing about NASDAQ stocks, Treasury securities, and any security issued by banks, trusts, S&L's, thrifts, credit unions, and building & loans.

So, I won't mention anything about them this time.

33. ANSWER: D

EXPLANATION: just memorize the question and the three answer choices. Isn't worth grappling with.

34. ANSWER: B

EXPLANATION: use your testing skills to the _max_ on this test. "Limited number" probably goes with the word "isolated." Then you link up the phrase "proceeds do not go to the issuer" with the words "non-issuer transaction," and your left with the phrase "isolated . .. non-issuer transaction." Plus the word "outstanding" was handed to you in the stem of the question.

If you choose an answer that matches up _that_ closely and it's somehow wrong, then NASAA is being way too tricky with their exams. And, believe it or not, NASAA swears they don't try to trick people taking the Series 63. Actually, they probably don't. It's just that the language they use is foreign to anyone who speaks English.

35. ANSWER: C

EXPLANATION: CFP's usually fall under the definition of Investment Adviser and have to register. They usually charge fees for managing money or putting together a detailed financial plan that usually involves *specific advice as to the value or advisability of investing in particular securities.*

Which means they usually fall neatly under the definition of an IA. NASAA has even gone out of its way to mention that most CFP's are defined as IA's and must register.

The other three choices are all specifically mentioned in the USA as not falling under the definition of IA . . . unless.

Unless the agent or broker-dealer does something crazy like try to charge a fee for their advice, or *Unless* the accountant makes her advice an integral component of her business, they are excluded from the definition of IA, which means there's one less hassle for them.

36. ANSWER: C

EXPLANATION: if the firm's only clients are insurance companies, they don't register at the state level. In fact, they don't even have to register with the SEC. I guess insurance companies are all considered big boys and girls who require very little protection. This, by the way, comes verbatim from the Investment Advisers Act of 1940, Section 203(b)(2).

Also note that if the adviser's only clients are registered investment companies, they register with the SEC—federal covered. So on the test if you see an IA in the state whose only clients are insurance companies, they don't register with anybody. And if their only clients are registered investment companies, they register with the SEC. So, more generally, if the IA's only clients are insurance and/or investment companies, they don't register at the state level.

Aren't you glad you know that?

37. ANSWER: D

EXPLANATION: agents have to be registered. Some securities do not. So, if you are an agent in Alabama, you have to register in Alabama, no matter what you sell. Some of the securities you sell will need to be registered, some will not. Either way, you—the agent—must register in the state of Alabama. So must your broker-dealer.

38. ANSWER: D

EXPLANATION: the question provides its own answer. Memorize the three answer choices and the general idea that the Administrator doesn't have to let the company issue securities in the state if the company is on shaky ground. This comes from the NASAA adopted policy statement on unsound financial condition cleverly titled "Unsound Financial Condition."

39. ANSWER: D

EXPLANATION: she has to disclose any securities-related violations over the past 10 years that got her in trouble with an Administrator, a court, or an SRO. If the misdemeanor is not related to securities or deceitful sales in general it does NOT need to be disclosed to the client. The disclosure, by the way, must be given 48 hours before entering into the advisory contract with the client. And, best of luck getting the client to sign on the dotted line after you drop that bomb!

40. ANSWER: D

EXPLANATION: the first three answer choices must be disclosed, but think of custody as an issue between the firm and the Administrator. The firm checks to see if the Administrator has a rule against taking custody. If not, they can take custody as long as they inform the Administrator in writing.

If the firm is in precarious financial condition or is/has been in trouble with the regulators, I'd say that's material (important, relevant) information for the client, right? Also, the client needs to know how much control the IA has over the account. Discretion means the firm can choose the activity, asset, or amount involved on any transaction even without contacting the client. That needs to be stipulated in the contract.

41. ANSWER: A

EXPLANATION: do you have discretion because your customer says she put the form in the mail? The regulators are real interested to see your instincts on this one.

No, you do not have discretion until you receive the power of attorney (trading authorization, discretionary authorization). An IA can actually go forward with verbal authorization as long as they get it in writing within 10 business days, but that seems trivial compared to how agents—folks like you—need to proceed. Don't use discretion until you have it in writing and your principal has signed off on the arrangement.

Price/time don't equal discretion, remember.

42. ANSWER: B

EXPLANATION: the number of accredited investors is unimportant. As usual, we're out to protect the little guys, the non-accredited investors. So, we can solicit all the accredited investors we want, but we can only sell to 10 or fewer non-accredited folks, and we can't get any commissions from those little guys. If the big guys plan to flip their shares, we don't worry so much about that and we can charge the big guys commissions. For the little guys, the seller might actually want a statement from them that they plan to hold these securities a while (buy for investment purposes). If they change their mind later and dump the shares, it's not automatically a problem, but the sooner they do it the worse it looks.

43. ANSWER: D

EXPLANATION: factoids for memorization, which you can get from NASAA's exciting statement of policy, called "Underwriting Expenses & Underwriting Warrants."

You should probably read this, unless, of course, you're waiting for the movie.

44. ANSWER: D

EXPLANATION: more factoids for memorization, which you can get from NASAA's lively work of prose entitled "Options and Warrants." You'll find it at www.nasaa.org under "nasaa library" adopted model rules.

45. ANSWER: B

EXPLANATION: only in "qualification" does the Big A have that much authority. In coordination, filing, and notice filing, the Big A is really just being informed. It's the SEC who plays the major role there.

46. ANSWER: C

EXPLANATION: the state of Ohio says that "rescission is a remedy, not a penalty." I like that. And, as Ohio says, the purpose is to make the client whole. If you get your money back, you've been made whole. Pain and suffering over a security?

Get a life.

The USA also states that the "cause of action survives death of both the plaintiff and the defendant." So if the investor dies, the kids can still come after you. If the rep dies, they can still go after the firm. The statute of limitations is basically two years from discovery of the alleged violation and never more than three years, even if the aggrieved party doesn't find out for 4 or 5. The criminal statue of limitations is 5 years, so there IS no 7-year statute for anything.

47. ANSWER: C

EXPLANATION: 60 days, not 15 or 30 or any other number. Also, the Administrative order is not immediately "stayed" (put on hold) just because you filed your appeal. In fact, it stays in effect unless and until the court decides otherwise. The court has the power to not just alter the Administrator's order but throw it out the window.

48. ANSWER: C

EXPLANATION: like most questions, this one is much easier than it looks. It just gives you more details than you probably care to take in, especially under pressure.

Okay, turn the tables on the question—what is it really asking? Where did the customer say *Sure, I'll take it*?

In Wyoming, so that's where the offer was accepted. Where payment is sent is irrelevant.

49. ANSWER: A

EXPLANATION: dumb people are still persons, and I don't know that an IQ of 110 qualifies as "dumb," anyway. By now you have surely memorized that anyone not dead, mentally incompetent, or a minor IS a legal person.

50. ANSWER: B

EXPLANATION: a cease & desist order can be issued even before the alleged violation occurs. You can also eliminate two choices. Habeas corpus is not on this exam. And the Administrator can NOT issue an injunction—only a court can do that. If he issues a cease & desist and these folks go ahead with their plans to sell the securities anyway, he'll get a court to issue an injunction.

Which is bad.

Why not a revocation? Because of the immediacy of the alleged violation. A revocation requires prior notice and an opportunity for a hearing. Too slow. The Big A wants to nip this thing in the bud—even before it buds, actually.

51. ANSWER: B

EXPLANATION: if you own a racehorse, you own a racehorse. That's not a security. It's a racehorse.

But a certificate of interest in a racehorse would be an investment contract, as defined by the Howey Decision, and investment contracts ARE securities. You can't forget the whiskey warehouse receipt even if you try at this point, right? And exclude the following insurance policies from the definition of security: term, whole life, endowment.

52. ANSWER: B

EXPLANATION: "secondary" means that the issuer does NOT get the proceeds. The former CEO gets the proceeds in choice B, so that's a "secondary" offering. The issuer in choice A gets the proceeds, so that's a primary, not a secondary, offering.

The real world gets this wrong every day. In the 'real world' people would often refer to choice A as a "secondary offering."

They would be wrong.

53. ANSWER: D

EXPLANATION: not worth explaining, although it might be worth reading the adopted statement of policy called "Preferred Stocks."

Or not.

54. ANSWER: C

EXPLANATION: "secondary" means that the issuer does NOT get the proceeds. The issuer in an IPO, subsequent primary offering, or a private placement gets the proceeds, so those are primary, not secondary, offerings.

55. ANSWER: D

EXPLANATION: the information has to be material, not immaterial, so you can eliminate choice I, which kills choices A and C with one stone. If you have to guess between willfully selling something you can't sell and using inside information, remember that using inside information is a prohibited act, not necessarily fraudulent. But, if you know the security should be registered but isn't, and you sell it anyway, now THAT's fraud.

Don't do that if you can help it.

56. ANSWER: B

EXPLANATION: misstating material facts when offering/selling securities and/or investment advice is just a textbook definition of fraud. The other stuff is merely prohibited.

57. ANSWER: D

EXPLANATION: take care of your customer before you take care of yourself.

Doesn't seem like so much to ask, does it? It's not fraud because you're not lying/deceiving your client. You're just doing something you shouldn't do.

Why shouldn't you do it? Because it's prohibited.

Did you enjoy all the irrelevant details about the customer's hobbies and pet pooch? The exam likes to distract you, too, so be prepared. You have to sift through the details, throwing out the immaterial in favor of the material information.

58. ANSWER: D

EXPLANATION: happy birthday from me

59. ANSWER: D

EXPLANATION: wow, now that was a hard question! Acting as a total weasel, I turned the tables on you. Usually when you see "with an office in the state," you know the firm has to register in the state. Except when they don't. If their only clients are insurance and/or registered investment companies, they don't register at the state level. And if their advice is only on Treasuries, they don't register, either.

Often when the firm has no office in the state, they aren't defined as IA's, but the de minimus exemption says the number of little guys (non-institutional clients) is 5 or fewer. With 9 little guys as clients the out-of-state IA will have to register in the other state.

Sorry about that.

60. ANSWER: C

EXPLANATION: choice C represents arbitrage, a difficult, risky, and totally acceptable trading strategy. The other stuff is bad and sounds bad, doesn't it?

REFERENCES

Glossary

adjudication: a determination made by a court of law

adjudication of mental incompetence: a court determines that a person is not competent mentally to make important decisions, no longer defined as a "legal person," unable to endorse certificates, open accounts

Administrator: the official or agency appointed by the Governor or state legislature to administer the USA in a state. Has the power to grant or take away licenses to sell securities and/or investment advice

agent: individual representing either a broker-dealer or a non-exempt issuer

aggrieved party: the person who has suffered grief over another person's alleged misdeeds

broker-dealer: a firm (sometimes an individual) in the business of completing transactions for others or for its own account.

cancellation: order entered by the Administrator when an applicant can not be located, has been declared mentally incompetent by a court of law, or stops doing business in the state. Not a punitive order—the applicant simply no longer exists as a business or legal entity in the state

cease & desist: order entered by the Administrator naming violations of registered persons and requiring the persons to cease and desist (refrain immediately) from engaging in such practices. If the affected person continues to engage in prohibited practices, an order to suspend or revoke the license/registration often follows

confirmation: a document *confirming* a transaction. These must be delivered to customers no later than settlement. For a new issue, the prospectus must be delivered with or before confirmation.

consent to service of process: a form that gives the Administrator the power to receive court papers on behalf of the person filing the consent

contempt: violating a court order

contumacy: disregarding an Administrator's order

convey for value a security: transfer a security for money or any other economic benefit

defraud: to deceive for financial gain

denial: order entered by the Administrator to deny an applicant's registration in the state. A punitive order resulting from the applicant's prior violations, injunctions, or unethical business practices

effect, as in "to *effect* a transaction": to complete

effective date: the date established by the SEC or the state securities Administrator as to when an issuer may release their securities for sale. Also called the release date

enjoin: to issue an injunction

exempt: not subject to; rules do not apply to

exempt transaction: the transaction is not subject to registration or filing of advertising materials. If the individual represents an issuer in an exempt transaction, the individual is not defined as an agent. Includes private placements, isolated non-issuer transactions in outstanding securities, transactions between an issuer and the underwriters, sales by fiduciaries, etc.

federal covered adviser: an adviser with not less than $25,000,000 of assets under management, or anyone (even with an office in the state) who advises a registered investment company, or whose sole clients are investment companies or insurance companies. Note that federal covered advisers still pay fees, provide notice, and file a consent to service of process with the state. But they're really under federal/ SEC jurisdiction.

federal covered security: a security not subject to the state's requirements for filing of advertising materials and registration. Any security exempt at the federal level or <u>covered</u> exclusively at the <u>federal</u> level, i.e. exchange-listed, NASDAQ stocks, investment company shares.

fiduciary: a person looking out for the benefit of another person

immaterial: not important, irrelevant

impoundment of proceeds: establishing an escrow account where proceeds from the offering of securities are impounded/not released to the issuer by the Administrator until the specified amount of money has been raised. Note that if the amount of money raised is insufficient, the proceeds (plus a pro rata share of the interest) goes to the investors, not the issuer or underwriters.

injunction: court order to prevent a person from doing something

insolvent: more liabilities than assets to pay 'em off with

institutional buyer: large investors such as mutual funds, pension funds, insurance companies, large trusts, banks, etc.

investment adviser: person (sometimes an individual) who charges a fee for providing investment advice as an integral part of their business

investment adviser representative: individual who represents an investment advisory firm by managing money, making recommendations, selling the services of the firm, or supervising anyone doing any of those advisory-type things.

issuer: anyone who issues or proposes to issue a security

market manipulation: an extremely exciting activity that will get you in more trouble than you bargained for. Includes words like: *pegging, capping, painting the tape, wash sales, matched purchases*

material: important, relevant, as in *material information may not be omitted or misstated in the purchase or sale of securities and/or investment advice*

non-exempt: has no exemption; rules <u>do</u> apply to

non-issuer transaction: not for the benefit of the issuer, a secondary offering, for example, where the proceeds of the sale go to a former CEO or board member, rather than the company itself

non-punitive termination: leaving a place of employment because you want to—not because you got in trouble

offer: an attempt to sell, or the attempt to get someone to make an offer to buy something

person: not dead, a minor, or mentally incompetent; a legal entity

preliminary prospectus: AKA "red herring". This is the prospectus before it's all completed. Doesn't have the final public offering price (POP) or the release date, because those haven't been determined yet.

primary market: the process of selling securities to investors in order to raise capital for issuers, i.e. IPO's and additional offerings

principal: a word with many meanings in the securities business. Principal is another name for the "par value" of a bond or the amount to be repaid on any debt against which interest is applied. The principal of a firm is a licensed supervisor responsible for the activities of sales representatives, customer complaints, record keeping, and financial reporting. And, to "act as a principal" in a transaction means to have money at risk, or to buy/sell for an inventory. When a broker-dealer acts as a dealer, it is acting as a principal. When an IA acts as a principal in a transaction with a customer, the firm is buying or selling the security for inventory. For IA's this activity must be disclosed and written customer consent must be obtained prior to the transaction

private placement: unregistered securities sold through an exemption to the Act of 1933. Securities are placed primarily in the hands of sophisticated investors, including officers and directors of the issuer, institutional buyers (mutual funds, insurance companies, pension funds), or accredited investors.

prospectus: a disclosure document that provides relevant, important, *material* facts about a security to a buyer

render, as in "to render advice regarding securities": to make and deliver

rescission: the act of rescinding, the act of "undoing" a transaction

rescind: to undo a transaction; the seller buys it back plus interest, less any income received from the security by the owner

revocation: an order entered by the Administrator taking away an existing license for a person or security

risk-averse: hates risk

sale/sell: a "contract" to dispose of a security for "value" (money, or any other economic benefit)

settlement: when the buyer of a security is officially recognized as the owner by the transfer agent. T + 3 for most securities, T + 1 for Treasury securities.

statute of limitations: the deadline for bringing criminal charges or civil suit against a person. For criminal cases, the deadline is five years; for civil action, the deadline is two years from discovery and never more than three years, regardless

subpoena: a court order or Administrative order to appear at a hearing/trial

suspension: exactly what it sounds like. A license for a broker-dealer, agent, investment adviser, or investment advisor has been suspended. A security's registration could also be suspended for reasons such as excessive underwriter compensation, insufficient disclosure, etc.

whiskey warehouse receipt: a security with no exemption and no aftertaste

withdrawal: the act of withdrawing an application for a person or security. The withdrawal is made by the person who had previously filed the registration. Effective as soon as the Administrator accepts it and no later than 30 days from receipt of the withdrawal, provided no orders to deny, suspend, or revoke are in place.

236

Index

Printed in the United States
36382LVS00001B/145-166

9 780912 301556